I0519848

Stories of Success:

Andy Grant's Pluck
(Illustrated)

Stories of Success:

Andy Grant's Pluck
(Illustrated)

Horatio Alger, Jr.

Sumner Books
Hermosa Beach, CA

Stories of Success:
Andy Grant's Pluck (Illustrated)
Copyright © 2015 Sumner Books
All rights reserved. No part of this book may be reproduced or transmitted in any form or by any means, electronic or mechanical, including photocopying, recording or by any information storage and retrieval system, without permission in writing from the author.

FIRST EDITION

Sumner Books

737 3rd St

Hermosa Beach, California 90254

310-337-7003

ISBN 978-1-939104-17-5

CREATORS PUBLISHING

TABLE OF CONTENTS

A NOTE FROM THE PUBLISHER

Horatio Alger helped form the American character, yet he is largely forgotten today. Those who are familiar with him think of the phrase, "rags to riches," but that's about it. Most young people have never even heard of him, even though at one time he was described as "America's most influential writer."

What an opportunity!

More than a hundred years before our contemporary self-help movement, Horatio Alger paved the way with his vivid illustrations of the keys to success and happiness. Today, Sumner Books is excited to introduce a new generation of Americans to some of the most inspirational stories ever written, what we call "Stories of Success." Regardless of your age, you simply cannot read a Horatio Alger book without coming away with a good feeling.

These books initially sold in the millions and then the tens of millions and finally the hundreds of millions. In fact, the Chicago Daily News once called Horatio Alger "America's best selling author of all time."

Sumner Books is committed to bringing to life this best selling collection in the form of audiobooks and e-books. For the first time ever, these "Stories of Success" will be bundled together as e-books when appropriate. Many times Horatio Alger wrote a novel that was well received, then he wrote three or four more novels over the next few years, and then came back to write Part II to the original novel. So we have taken the two novels that follow the same characters and interwoven plots and published them as a single e-book.

All of the "Stories of Success" e-books offer a detailed table of contents, colored illustrations, commentary and a teacher's guide. They are professionally edited, including the occasional updating of phrases to make the books as easy to read today as they were when they were first published between 1865 and 1900.

Long after his death in 1899, the magazine Publishers Weekly wrote: "To call Horatio Alger Jr. America's most influential writer may seem like an overstatement ... but ... only Benjamin Franklin meant as much to the formation of the American popular mind."

Our goal is to bring back some of the influence that Alger exerted on millions of young people in America. Yes, it's retro; it's counterintuitive and totally contrary to the cynicism that has become a part of American culture. But we are proud to be leading a movement that is as positive and uplifting as the last pages of a Horatio Alger story.

Rick Newcombe
President
Sumner Books

Stories of Success

"Try not to become a man of success but rather try to become a man of value."
Albert Einstein

CHAPTER I

THE TELEGRAM

"A telegram for you, Andy!" said Arthur Bacon as he entered the room of Andy Grant in Penhurst Academy.

"A telegram!" repeated Andy in vague alarm, for the word suggested something urgent -- probably bad news of some kind.

He tore open the envelope and read the few words of the message:

Come home at once. Something has happened.

MOTHER.

"What can it be?" thought Andy perplexed. "At any rate, mother is well, for she sent the telegram."

"What is it?" asked Arthur.

"I don't know. You can read the telegram for yourself."

"Must you go home?" asked Arthur in a tone of regret.

"Yes. When is there a train?"

"At three this afternoon."

"I will take it. I must go and see Dr. Crabb."

"But won't you come back again?"

"I don't know. I am all in the dark. I think something must have happened to my father."

Dr. Crabb was at his desk in his library -- it was Saturday afternoon, and school was not in session -- when Andy knocked at the door.

"Come in!" said the doctor in a deep voice.

Andy opened the door and entered. Dr. Crabb smiled, for Andy was his favorite pupil.

"Come in, Grant!" he said. "What can I do for you?"

"Give me permission to go home. I have just had a telegram. I will show it to you."

The doctor was a man of fifty-five, with a high forehead and an intellectual face. He wore glasses and had done so for ten years. They gave him the appearance of a learned scholar, as he was.

"Dear me!" he said. "How unfortunate! Only two weeks to the end of the term, and you are our primus!"

"I am very sorry, sir, but perhaps I may be able to come back."

"Do so, by all means, if you can. There is hardly a pupil I could not better spare."

"Thank you, sir," said Andy gratefully. "There is a train at three o'clock. I would like to take it."

"By all means. And let me hear from you, even if you can't come back."

"I will certainly write, doctor. Thank you for all your kindness."

Penhurst Academy was an endowed school. On account of the endowments, the annual rate to boarding scholars was very reasonable -- only three hundred dollars, including everything.

A school in Connecticut in the early 1900s.

The academy had a fine reputation, which it owed in large part to the high character and gifts of Dr. Crabb, who had been the principal for twenty-five years. He had connected himself with the school soon after he left Dartmouth and had been identified with it for the greater part of his active life.

Andy had been a pupil for over two years and was an excellent Latin and Greek scholar. In a few months he would be ready for college.

Dr. Crabb was anxious to have him go to Dartmouth, his own alma mater, being convinced that he would do him credit and make a brilliant record for scholarship. Indeed, it was settled that he would go, his parents being ready to be guided by the doctor's advice.

From Penhurst to Arden, where Andy's parents lived, was fifty miles. Starting at three o'clock, the train reached Arden station at five.

As Andy stepped on the platform he saw Roland Hunter, the son of a neighbor.

"How are you, Andy?" said Roland with a cheerful greeting. "How do you happen to be coming home? Is it vacation?"

"No. I was summoned home by a telegram. Is -- are they all well at home?"

"Yes, so far as I know."

Andy breathed a sigh of relief.

"I am glad of that," he said. "I was afraid someone in the family might be sick."

"I don't think so. I would have heard, living so near."

"Father is well, then?"

"Come to think of it, I heard he had a bad headache."

"At any rate, it isn't anything serious. Are you going home? If you are, I'll walk along with you."

"We can do better than that. I've got uncle's buggy on the other side of the depot. I'll take you, bag and baggage."

"Thank you, Roland. My bag is rather heavy, and as it is a mile to the house, I shall be glad to accept your offer."

"Bundle in, then," said Roland merrily. "I don't know but I ought to charge you a quarter. That's the regular fare by stage."

"All right! Charge it if you like," rejoined Andy smiling. "Are your folks all well?"

"Oh, yes, especially Lily. You and she are great friends, I believe."

"Oh, yes," answered Andy with a smile.

"She thinks a good deal more of you than she does of me."

"Girls don't generally appreciate their brothers, I believe. If I had a sister, I presume she would like you better than me."

Roland dropped Andy at his father's gate.

It may be said here that Mr. Grant owned a farm of fifty acres that yielded him a comfortable living when supplemented by the interest on three thousand dollars invested in government bonds. On the farm was a house of moderate size which had always been a pleasant home to Andy and his little brother Robert, generally called Robbie.

Andy opened the gate and walked up to the front door, valise in hand.

The house and everything about it seemed just as it did when he left at the beginning of the school term. But Andy looked at them with different eyes.

Then he had been in good spirits, eager to return to his school work. Now something had happened, but he did not yet know what.

Mrs. Grant was in the back part of the house, and Andy was in the sitting room before she was fully aware of his presence. Then she came in from the kitchen, where she was preparing supper.

Her face seemed careworn, but there was a smile upon it as she greeted her son.

"Then you got my telegram?" she said. "I didn't think you would be here so soon."

"I started at once, mother, for I felt anxious. What has happened? Are you all well?"

"Yes, thank God, we are in fair health, but we have met with misfortune."

"What is it?"

"Nathan Lawrence, cashier of the bank in Benton, has disappeared with twenty thousand dollars of the bank's money."

"What has that to do with father? He hasn't much money in that bank."

"Your father is on Mr. Lawrence's bond to the amount of six thousand dollars."

"I see," answered Andy gravely. "How much will he lose?"

"The whole of it."

This, then, was what had happened. To a man in moderate circumstances, it was a heavy blow.

"I suppose it will make a great difference?" said Andy inquiringly.

"You can judge. Your father's property consists of this farm and three thousand dollars in government bonds. It will be necessary to sacrifice the bonds and place a mortgage of three thousand dollars on the farm."

"How much is the farm worth?"

"Not over six thousand dollars."

"Then father's property is nearly all swept away."

"Yes," said his mother sadly. "Hereafter he will receive no help from outside interest and will, besides, have to pay interest on a mortgage of three thousand dollars, at six per cent."

"One hundred and eighty dollars."

"Yes."

"Altogether, then, it will diminish our income by rather more than three hundred dollars."

"Yes, Andy."

"That is about what my education has been costing father," said Andy in a low voice.

He began to see how this misfortune was going to affect him.

"I am afraid," faltered Mrs. Grant, "that you will have to leave school."

"Of course I must," said Andy, speaking with a cheerfulness which he did not feel. "And in place of going to college I must see how I can help father bear this burden."

"It will be very hard upon you, Andy," said his mother in a tone of sympathy.

"I shall be sorry, of course, mother, but there are plenty of boys who don't go to college. I shall be no worse off than they."

"I am glad you bear the disappointment so well, Andy. It is of you your father and I have thought chiefly since the blow fell upon us."

"Who will advance father the money on mortgage, mother?"

"Squire Carter has expressed a willingness to do so. He will be here this evening to talk it over."

"I am sorry for that, mother. He is a hard man. If there is a chance to take advantage of father, he won't hesitate to do it."

CHAPTER II

SQUIRE CARTER

When Mr. Grant entered the room, he seemed to Andy to have grown five years older. His face was sad, and he had lost the brisk, cheerful manner which was habitual to him.

"Has your mother told you?" he asked.

"Yes, father." Then he added with indignation, "What a wicked man Mr. Lawrence must be!"

"I suppose he was tempted," said Mr. Grant slowly. "Here is a note I received from him this morning."

Andy took the envelope from his father's hand and, opening it, read the following lines:

OLD FRIEND:

Perhaps by the time you receive this letter you will have heard of the wrong I have done you and yours, and the loss I have brought upon you. It is to me a source of the greatest sorrow, for I fear you will never recover from it. I am just ready to go away. I cannot stay here to receive punishment, for it would tie my hands and prevent my making reparation, as I hope some day to do. Why did I go wrong? I can't explain, except that it was infatuation. In a moment of madness I took some of the funds of the bank and risked them on Wall Street. I lost and went in deeper, hoping to be more fortunate and replace the stolen money. That is the way such things usually happen.

I can say no more, except that it will be my earnest effort to give you back the money you will lose by me. It may take years, but I hope we both shall live long enough for me to do it.

NATHAN LAWRENCE.

Andy read this letter in silence and gave it back to his father.

"Do you believe he is sincere?" he asked.

"Yes, he has many good points, and I believe he really feels attached to me."

"He has taken a strange way to show it."

"He was weak and yielded to temptation. There are many like him."

"Do you believe he will ever be able to make up the loss?"

"I don't know. He is a man of fine business talent and may be able in time to do something, but his defalcation amounts to twenty thousand dollars."

"We must try to make the best of it, father. You have been spending three hundred dollars a year for me, besides the expense of my clothes. If that is saved, it will make up your loss of income."

"But, my dear boy, I don't like to sacrifice your prospects."

"It won't be sacrificing them," said Andy with forced cheerfulness. "It will only change them. Of course, I must give up the thought of a college education, but I may make a success in business."

"It will be very hard upon you," said Mr. Grant sadly.

"No, father. I won't deny that I shall be sorry just at first, but it may turn out better for me in the end."

"You are a good boy, to take it so well, Andy. I had no right to risk so much, even for a friend like Lawrence."

"You have known Mr. Lawrence for many years, have you not, father?"

"Yes. We were schoolboys together. I thought him the soul of honor. But I ought not to have risked three-quarters of my estate, even for him."

"You can't be blamed, father. You had full confidence in him."

"Yes, I had full confidence in him," sighed Mr. Grant.

"And he may yet be able to make up the loss to you."

Though Andy said this, he only said it to mitigate his father's regret, for he had very little confidence in the missing cashier or his promises. He was repaid by seeing his father brighten up.

"You have cheered me, Andy," he said. "I don't care so much for myself, but I have been thinking of you and your mother."

"And we have been thinking of you, father," said Mrs. Grant. "It might be worse."

"I don't see very well how that could be."

"We are in good health, thank God! And your reputation is unblemished. Compare your position with that of Nathan Lawrence, forced to flee in disgrace under a load of shame."

"You are right, dear. He is more to be pitied than I am."

"Is he a married man, father?"

"No. That is, he is a widower."

"While we are spared to each other, we must trust in God and hope for the best."

"Mother tells me you expect to get part of the money you need from Squire Carter," said Andy.

"Yes, he has promised to take a mortgage of three thousand dollars on the old place."

"I have heard he is a hard man, father. I don't think he is influenced by kindness."

"I can't afford to inquire into his motives. It is enough that he will furnish the money. But for that I might have to sell the farm, and then we should be quite helpless."

About seven o'clock Squire Carter made his appearance. Andy opened the door for him.

He was a tall, florid-faced man, with an air of consequence based upon his knowledge that he was the richest man in the town.

"Good evening, Andrew," he said, for he was always formal. "So you are home from school?"

"Yes, sir."

"When did you come?"

"This afternoon, sir."

"I suppose you heard of your father's misfortune?"

"Yes, sir."

"Ha! It is very sad -- very sad, indeed. I quite feel for your father. I am trying to help him out of his trouble. He was a very foolish man to risk so much on that rascal, Lawrence."

Andy was disposed to agree with the squire, but he did not like to hear his father blamed.

"I think he realizes that he was unwise, Squire Carter," said Andy. "Won't you walk in?"

"I suppose your father is at home?" said the squire as he stepped into the front entry.

"Yes, sir. He was expecting you."

Andy opened the door of the sitting room, and the squire entered. Mr. Grant rose from the rocking chair in which he was seated and welcomed his visitor.

"I am glad to see you, squire," he said. "Take a seat by the fire."

"Thank you," said the squire with dignity. "I came, as I said I would. I do not desert an old neighbor because he has been unfortunate."

But for his patronizing tone his words would have awakened more gratitude. As it was, his manner seemed to say, "See how kind-hearted I am."

Somehow, Andy felt more and more sorry to think his father must be indebted to such a man.

"It is getting quite fallish," said the squire rubbing his hands. "I suppose I am more sensitive to cold, as my home is heated throughout with steam."

"I hope we shall be able to make you comfortable, Squire Carter," returned Mrs. Grant, who had entered the room in time to hear this last speech.

"Oh, yes, Mrs. Grant. I always adapt myself to circumstances."

"That is very kind of you," Andy was tempted to say, but he forbore. It would not do to offend the village magnate.

"I see you have sent for Andrew," observed the squire with a wave of his hand toward the boy.

"Yes. I shall not be able to keep him at Penhurst Academy any longer."

"Very sensible decision of yours. No doubt it cost you a pretty penny to keep him there?"

"The school charge is three hundred dollars a year."

"Bless my soul! How extravagant! You will excuse my saying so, but I think you have been very unwise. It really seems like a wasteful use of money."

"Don't you believe in education, squire?" asked Mrs. Grant.

"Yes, but why couldn't he get all the education he needs here?"

"Because there is no one here who teaches Latin and Greek."

"And what good would Latin and Greek do him? I don't know anything of Latin and Greek, and yet I flatter myself I have succeeded pretty well. I believe I am looked up to in the village, eh?"

"No doubt you occupy a prominent position, squire, but the boy had a fancy for the languages and wanted to go to college."

"I shall not send my son to college, though of course I can afford it."

"Perhaps he doesn't care to go."

"No, the boy is sensible. He will be satisfied with the advantages his father enjoyed. Supposing your boy had gone to college, what would you have made of him?"

"He thought he would have liked to prepare himself to become a teacher or professor."

"It's a poor business, Neighbor Grant. A schoolmate of mine became a teacher -- the teacher of an academy -- and I give you my word, he's as poor as poverty."

13

"Money isn't everything, squire."

"It's a good deal, as in your present circumstances you must admit. But we may as well come to business."

CHAPTER III

ANDY LEAVES THE ACADEMY

"You need to raise three thousand dollars, I believe, Neighbor Grant?" began the squire.

"Yes, squire."

"Three thousand dollars is a good deal of money."

"I realize that," said Mr. Grant sadly.

"I was about to say it is a good deal to raise on the security of the farm."

"The farm cost me six thousand dollars."

"It would fetch only five thousand now. It wouldn't fetch that at a forced sale."

"But for my losses, I wouldn't consider an offer of less than six thousand."

"Of course, you are attached to it, and that gives it a fancy value in your eyes."

"It is good land and productive. Then, it is well situated, and the buildings are good."

"Well, tolerable," said the squire cautiously. "However, that's neither here nor there. You want three thousand dollars, and I have agreed to let you have it. I will take a mortgage for two years, the interest being, as usual, six per cent."

"Two years?" repeated Farmer Grant uneasily.

"Yes. I am not sure that I can spare the money longer than two years. I give you that time to pay it off."

"But it will be impossible for me to pay it off in two years. In fact, it will take all my income to live and pay the interest."

"Of course that isn't my concern."

"Do you mean that you will foreclose in two years?"

"Not necessarily. I may not need the money so soon. Besides, you may find some one else to take it off my hands."

"Can't you say five years, squire?" pleaded the farmer.

Squire Carter shook his head.

"No. You can take it or leave it. I am not at all anxious to take the mortgage, and if my terms are not agreeable, we will consider the negotiations at an end."

"I won't make any difficulty, squire. I accept your terms."

"That is sensible. I can't, for my part, see how five years would have been more favorable to you than two."

"My son Andrew is sixteen. By the time he is twenty-one he might help me."

"There's not much chance of that -- unless he marries a fortune," said the squire jocosely. "I suppose you will keep him at home to help you on the farm?"

"We haven't talked the matter over yet. I will consult his wishes as far as I can. He can't earn much money on the farm. What are you going to do with your son?"

"Conrad will probably be a merchant, or a banker," said the squire pompously.

"With your means you can select any path in life for him."

"True. As my son he will have a great advantage. Well, as our business is arranged, I will leave you. If you will call at Lawyer Tower's office tomorrow at noon the papers can be drawn up, and I will give you a check for the money."

"Thank you, squire. I will meet the appointment."

"If you don't want Andrew to work on the farm I will turn over his case in my mind and see if I can get him a position."

"Thank you. I should be glad to have him well started in some business where he can raise himself."

As the term of the academy was so nearly completed, Andy went back with his father's permission, to remain till vacation. He sought an interview at once with Dr. Crabb, the principal, and informed him of the necessity he was under of leaving the institution.

"I am really sorry, Andrew," said the doctor. "You are one of my best pupils. I am not sure but the best. There is scarcely one that I would not sooner lose. I shall be willing to take you for half price -- that is, for one hundred and fifty dollars -- till you are ready for college."

"Thank you, Dr. Crabb," replied Andy gratefully. "You are very kind, but even that sum my father, in his changed circumstances, would be unable to pay. Besides, it would be quite out of my power to go to college even if I were prepared."

"It is a thousand pities," said the principal with concern. "If you must leave, you must. I am not sure but I should be willing to take you gratuitously."

"Thank you, but I feel that I ought to go to work at once to help my father. It is not enough that I free him from expense."

"No doubt you are right. I respect you for your determination. You need not hesitate to apply to me at any time in the future if you see any way in which I can be of service to you."

"I think it will help me if you will give me a letter of recommendation, which I can show to any one from whom I seek employment."

"I will give you such a letter with great pleasure," and the doctor, sitting down at his desk, wrote a first-class recommendation of his favorite pupil.

There was general regret in the academy when it was learned that Andy must leave them. One little boy of twelve -- Dudley Cameron, a special favorite of Andy -- came to him to ask if there was no way by which he could manage to stay.

"No, Dudley! I am too poor," said Andy.

"If I write to papa and ask him to send you a thousand dollars, will you stay?" asked the little boy, earnestly.

"No, Dudley. You mustn't do anything of the kind. Even if your father liked me as well as you do, and would give me the money, I could not take it. I must go to work to help my father."

"You will write to me sometimes, Andy?"

"Yes, I will be sure to do that."

The little fellow's warm-hearted offer, and the expressions of sympathy and regret on the part of his schoolmates, cheered Andy. It was pleasant to think that he would be missed.

On the closing day he received the first prize for scholarship from the hands of Dr. Crabb.

"You will take my best wishes with you, Andy," said the venerable principal. "Let me hear from you when you have made any business arrangement."

The farewells were said, and Andy set out on his return home.

He was leaving the old life behind him. A new one lay before him, but what it was to be he could not foresee.

A small town outside of New York City, around the 1870s.

He reached Arden in due course and set out to walk home. He had barely started when he heard his name called.

Looking around, he saw Conrad Carter, the squire's only son, on his bicycle.

"So you've come home from the academy?" said Conrad curiously.

"Yes," answered Andy briefly.

He never could bring himself to like Conrad, who made himself offensive and unpopular by his airs of superiority. Indeed, there was no boy in Arden so thoroughly disliked as Conrad.

"You'll have a pretty long vacation," went on Conrad with a significant laugh.

"Yes, I suppose so."

"Oh, well, it's the best thing for you. I thought it foolish when your father sent you off to the academy. If the Arden grammar school is good enough for me it is good enough for you."

"There is nothing to prevent your going to the academy."

"I know that. My father could afford it, even if it cost a good deal more. You wanted to go to college, didn't you?"

"Yes."

"It was very foolish for a poor boy like you."

"Of course your age and experience make your opinion of value," said Andy with a sarcasm which he did not care to conceal.

"I advise you not to be too independent," returned Conrad displeased. "Are you going to work on the farm?"

"I may till I get a situation."

"I'll speak to father. He might take you for an errand boy."

"I don't think that place would suit me."

"Why not?"

"I want to go into some mercantile establishment and learn business."

"That's what I am going to do when I get through school. Of course there is no hurry in my case."

"I suppose not."

"I suppose you know that my father has taken a mortgage on your father's farm?"

"Yes, I know that."

"If your father can't pay the mortgage when it is due, father will have to take the farm."

Andy made no answer, but thought Conrad more disagreeable than ever. By way of changing the conversation, he said:

"That's a new bicycle, isn't it?"

"Yes, I got tired of the old one. This is a very expensive one. Wouldn't you like to own a bicycle?"

"Yes."

"Of course, you never will."

"Then I must be content without one."

"Well, I must leave you. I'll come around soon and see you ride a horse to plow."

As Conrad sped away on his wheel, Andy said to himself, "I shouldn't like to be rich if it made me as disagreeable as Conrad."

CHAPTER IV

PREPARING FOR THE PICNIC

The change in his father's circumstances had come so suddenly that Andy could not immediately decide upon a plan of securing employment.

He was not idle, however. There was work to do on the farm, and he took off his uniform -- for Penhurst Academy was a military school -- and donned, instead, a rough farm suit, in which he assisted his father.

If he felt a pang of regret he did not show it, for he did not wish to add to his father's grief over his imprudent act of friendship.

It was while he was at work hoeing corn that Conrad Carter came up one day and leaning against the fence, looked at Andy with an amused expression.

"Oho, you've turned farmer in earnest!" he said.

"Yes, for the time being," answered Andy composedly.

"You look fine in your overalls."

"Do you think so? Thank you for the compliment."

"You might as well keep on. You will probably succeed better as a farmer than in business."

"I mean to succeed in anything I undertake."

"You've got a comfortable opinion of yourself."

"While you, on the contrary, are modest and unassuming."

"What do you mean?" asked Conrad coloring.

"I meant to compliment you, but if you don't like it I will take it back. Suppose I say that you are neither modest nor unassuming."

"If that is the way you are going to talk to me I will go away," said Conrad haughtily. "It is a little imprudent, considering -- "

"Considering what?"

"That my father can turn you all out at the end of two years."

"If that is the way you are going to talk to me I shall be glad to have you go away, as you just threatened."

"Pride and poverty don't go together very well," said Conrad, provoked.

"I don't want to be either proud or poor," returned Andy smiling.

"That fellow provokes me," thought Conrad. "However, he'll repent it some time."

In five minutes his place was taken by Valentine Burns, an intimate friend of Andy's. His father kept the village store and was one of the leading citizens of Arden.

"Hard at work, I see, Andy," he said.

"Don't you want to help me?"

"No, I'm too lazy. I have to work in the store out of school hours, you know. Are you going to the picnic?"

"What picnic?"

"There's a Sunday school picnic next Thursday afternoon. Both churches unite in it. All the young people will be there. You would have heard of it if you hadn't been absent at school."

"I will certainly go. There are so few amusements in Arden that I can't afford to miss any. I suppose there will be the usual attractions?"

"Yes, and an extra one besides. There's a gentleman from the city staying at the hotel who has offered a prize of ten dollars to the boy who will row across the pond in the shortest time."

"The distance is about half a mile, isn't it?"

"Yes, a little more."

"I suppose you will go in for the prize, Val. You have a nice boat to practice in."

"No amount of practice would give me the prize. I don't excel as a rower."

"Who is expected to win?"

"Conrad Carter confidently counts on securing the prize. There is no boy in Arden that can compete with him, except -- "

"Well, except whom?"

"Andy Grant."

"I don't know," said Andy thoughtfully. "I can row pretty well -- that is, I used to -- but I am out of practice."

"Why don't you get back your practice?"

"I have no boat."

"Then use mine," said Valentine promptly.

"You are very kind, Val. How many days are there before the picnic?"

"Five. In five days you can accomplish a great deal."

"I should like to win the ten dollars. I want to go to the city and look for a place, and I don't want to ask father for the money."

"Ten dollars would carry you there nicely. and give you a day or two to look around."

"True. Well, Val, I will accept your kind offer. Is Conrad practicing?"

"Yes, he is out every afternoon."

"I can't go till after supper."

"Then begin this evening. You know where I keep my boat. I will be at the boathouse at half-past six, and you can meet me there."

"All right. You are a good friend, Val."

"I try to be, but it isn't all friendship."

"What else, then?"

"I want Conrad defeated. He is insufferable now, and if he wins the prize he will be worse than ever."

Prospect Pond was a little distance out of the village. It was a beautiful sheet of water, and a favorite resort for picnic parties. Conrad Carter, Valentine Burns, and two or three other boys and young men had boats there, and a man named Serwin kept boats to hire.

But the best boats belonged to Valentine and Conrad. It was rather annoying to Conrad that anyone should have a boat as good as his own, but this was something he could not help. He consoled himself, however, by reflecting that he was a better oarsman than Valentine.

He had been out practicing during the afternoon, accompanied by John Larkin, a neighbor's son. John stood on the bank and timed him.

"Well, John, how do I row?" he asked when he returned from his trial trip.

"You did very well," said John.

"There won't be anyone else that can row against me, eh?"

"I can't think of anyone. Valentine has as good a boat -- "

"I don't admit that," said Conrad jealously.

"I would just as soon have his as yours," said John independently, "but he can't row with you."

"I should think not."

"Jimmy Morris is a pretty good rower, but he has no boat of his own and would have to row in one of Serwin's boats. You know what they are."

"He couldn't come up to me, no matter in what boat he rowed," said Conrad.

"Well, perhaps not. I don't know."

"Well, you ought to know, John Larkin."

"My opinion's my own, Conrad," said John manfully.

"All the same, you are mistaken."

"If Valentine would lend his boat to Jimmy we could tell better."

"He won't do it. He will want it himself," said Conrad.

"As matters stand now, I think you will win the prize."

"I think so myself."

It may be thought surprising that nothing was said of Andy Grant and his chances, but, in truth, his friends in Arden had never seen him row during the last two years.

As a matter of fact, he had been the champion oarsman of Penhurst Academy, but this they did not know. During his vacations at home he had done very little rowing, his time being taken up in other ways.

"I wonder whether Andy Grant can row?" said John Larkin.

Conrad laughed.

"He can hoe corn and potatoes better than he can row, I fancy," he said.

"He's a first-rate fellow," said Larkin warmly.

"He's poor and proud, that's what he is. I called at the farm this morning and he insulted me."

"Are you sure it wasn't the other way?"

"Look here, John Larkin. If you don't treat me with more respect I won't associate with you."

"Do as you like," said John independently. "I'd just as soon associate with Valentine or Andy."

"My father can buy out both their fathers."

"That don't make you any the better fellow. Why are you so anxious to win this prize? Is it the money you are after?"

"No. If I want ten dollars my father will give it to me. It isn't the money, but the glory that I think of."

"If I had your practice I'd go for it myself. I shouldn't mind pocketing ten dollars."

"No doubt it would be welcome to you."

"Let me try your boat for a few minutes."

"You can have it for ten minutes."

"I would like it long enough to row over the course."

"You can have it that long. I'm going over it again myself as soon as I have got rested from the last trial."

John Larkin got into the boat and rowed very creditably, but was soon called in by the owner of the craft.

John began to ask himself what benefit he got from associating with Conrad, who showed his selfishness on all occasions.

"I wish he would get beaten, after all," thought John, "but I don't know who there is to do it. Valentine is only a passable rower, and Jimmy Morris has no boat of his own."

Conrad came back in good spirits. He had beaten his former record by three-quarters of a minute.

"I'm sure of the prize," he said, in exultation.

CHAPTER V

THE BOAT RACE

As Andy rowed only in the evening and Conrad practiced in the afternoon, it chanced that the coming rivals never met; nor was Conrad aware that Andy proposed to dispute the prize with him.

Even at first Valentine was surprised and pleased to observe how Andy handled the oars. Before the evening was over he demonstrated the fact that he was a first-class oarsman, much to the satisfaction of his friend.

"You must have had a good deal of practice at the gymnasium," said Valentine.

"Yes. The director of the gymnasium, who is an all-around athlete, gave the boys special instruction, by which we all profited. He was a graduate of Harvard, and an old member of the University crew."

"That accounts for it. Your rowing has a style to it that Conrad cannot show."

"Probably he has never had any instructions."

"Whatever he has accomplished has come by practice. He pulls a strong oar, but there is a roughness and lack of smoothness about his work. Still, he gets over the water pretty fast."

"And that counts. How does his speed compare with mine?"

"As you rowed tonight, I think the race would be a close one. But this is only the first evening. Keep on practicing daily, and I will bet on you every time."

Andy looked pleased.

"I am glad to hear you say this," he said. "I shall not row for glory, but for the ten dollars, which I shall find very useful. You have a fine boat, Val. How does Conrad's compare with yours?"

"I should hardly know how to choose between them. His boat is a fine one, but mine is quite as good."

"And I suppose there is no other on the pond as fine."

"No. Serwin's boats are old style and have been in use for years. If you rowed in one of those against Conrad you would be sure to be beaten."

"Then if I win I shall be indebted to you for the victory."

Valentine smiled.

"I should be glad to think I had anything to do with gaining the prize for you, even indirectly, but it will be due in large measure to your own good rowing. Only, keep up your practicing."

"I will do so."

"I want you to win; and, besides, I want Conrad to lose. I hope he won't hear anything of your entering the race."

Two days before the picnic Valentine happened to meet Conrad at his father's store.

"Are you going to enter the boat race at the picnic?" asked the latter.

"I am not certain."

"You have the only boat that can compare with mine. Have you been practicing any?"

"I have been rowing a little."

"I shall have to look out," said Conrad, but his manner did not indicate apprehension. "Probably the prize will go either to you or me."

"Thank you for the compliment."

"Suppose we have a little trial by ourselves? It may do us both good."

"I don't mind. When shall it be?"

"Say tomorrow afternoon."

"Very well. I will be at the pond at four o'clock."

"All right."

The two boys met according to agreement, and the race took place.

Conrad won easily by eight lengths, although Valentine exerted himself to the best of his ability.

"That settles it," said Conrad, triumphantly. "You can't row against me."

"I am afraid you are right," returned Valentine with an air of chagrin.

"You will need more practice, though you row fairly well. I think you pull the best oar next to me," said Conrad in a patronizing tone.

"Yes, I see that I must practice more."

"There will be no need for me to practice," said Conrad to himself. "I've got a dead sure thing."

It might have been supposed that Conrad would be indifferent to the money value of the prize offered, but he had extravagant tastes and found his allowance from his father, though a liberal one, insufficient for his needs. He began to consider in what way he would spend the money, which he considered as good as won.

At length the day for the picnic dawned. The day previous had been unpleasant, and there had been considerable anxiety lest the weather should prove unpleasant. But greatly to the general satisfaction it was bright with sunshine, and the temperature was delightful.

The young people of both societies turned out en masse and looked forward to a good time.

**The townspeople from Arden gather for a picnic
and to watch the boat race.
("The Picnic" by Thomas Cole)**

The race had been fixed for half-past three o'clock. At that hour the superintendent of the Sunday school came forward and said, "Owing to the generosity of Mr. Gale, of New York, a boarder at the hotel, a prize of ten dollars has been offered to the best oarsman who may compete for it. Boats will start from the pier, and the course will be to the opposite bank of the pond and back. I am sure that this will prove a very attractive feature of our picnic. Boys who intend to compete will now present themselves."

The first to come forward was Conrad Carter. He was dressed in a handsome boating costume, and his manner indicated great confidence. He looked around for Valentine, but the latter made no motion toward the shore, though his boat was in the pond drawn up with the rest.

"Aren't you going to row, Valentine?" asked Conrad in surprise.

"No, I have lent my boat to Andy Grant."

At the same time Andy, in his ordinary attire, came forward and stepped into Valentine's boat.

Conrad arched his brows in surprise. He had been disappointed to find that Valentine would not row, but he was quite as well pleased at the prospect of beating Andy.

He was rather surprised, however, as he had never heard that Andy could row.

"He must be a fool to think of rowing against me," he said to himself.

Next came Jimmy Morris, who took his place in one of Serwin's boats.

Two other boys also appeared in hired boats, one of them being Dennis Carlyle, a friend of John Larkin.

When the boats were in line, a superintendent gave the signal.

Conrad got the first start. The others kept together, a length or two behind Conrad. Andy did not appear to be exerting himself, but his strokes showed a smoothness that was lacking in any of the rest.

Mr. Gale, the donor of the prize, who was himself a good rower, took notice of him.

"Who is that boy?" he asked pointing to Andy. "I don't think I have seen him before."

"It is Andy Grant, the son of Farmer Grant."

"Why haven't I seen him before?"

"He has been absent at school -- at Penhurst Academy."

"He knows how to row. See how he handles his oars."

"I didn't know he was a rower."

"He is, and a good one. I shouldn't be surprised if he wins the race."

"What, against Conrad Carter?" asked the superintendent incredulously.

"Yes. It is easy to see that he has been trained, while Conrad, though he pulls a strong oar, rows like a country amateur."

Conrad was so intent upon his own work that he had not had an opportunity of watching his competitors. When he had nearly reached the point selected on the other bank, he turned about and saw Andy close behind him.

Andy was not apparently exerting himself but pulled a strong, steady stroke, and seemed quite free from excitement. For the first time Conrad saw that he was a competitor not to be despised.

After the turn Conrad and Andy led the procession. Next came Jimmy Morris and last of all Dennis Carlyle.

The latter managed to catch a crab, or dig his oar blade into the water at the wrong moment, and in his attempt to right himself he tumbled into the water.

"Don't mind me!" he called out humorously. "I am only taking a bath."

So the other contestants kept on, in the same order.

But this was not to continue. Suddenly Andy made a spurt and forged ahead of Conrad. The young aristocrat could hardly believe his eyes when he saw Valentine's boat, impelled by a competitor whom he had despised, take the leading place.

He flushed with vexation and made a desperate effort to regain his lost position. But he was excited and did not use his strength to the best advantage.

To his great annoyance he saw that Andy was continuing to gain upon him, and he was doing so without any great effort. His smooth, steady stroke was most effective. Even the unpracticed eye could see his superiority to any of his competitors.

When the goal was reached he was five lengths ahead of Conrad and twelve lengths ahead of Jimmy Morris.

It was a genuine surprise to the spectators, and a great shout went up.

"Three cheers for Andy Grant!"

Andy smiled, and he raised his hat in acknowledgment of the compliment.

Mr. Gale pressed forward and greeted the young victor.

"You have done yourself credit," he said. "You know how to row. Where did you learn?"

"At Penhurst Academy. I was trained by a Harvard oarsman."

"He understood his business, and so do you. I have great pleasure in presenting you with the prize."

With a sullen look Conrad listened to those words. Without a word he sprang on shore and, as soon as he could, turned his back upon the picnic.

"Conrad is terribly disappointed!" said Valentine. "You have made yourself famous, Andy."

CHAPTER VI

A LIBERAL OFFER

Thoroughly mortified and crestfallen, Conrad went home. He hoped to go up to his room without observation, but his father noticed his entrance.

"Well, Conrad," he said with a smile, "did you carry off the honors at the picnic?"

"No, I didn't," answered Conrad bitterly.

"Did Valentine Burns defeat you?"

"No."

"Who did win the prize?"

"Andy Grant."

Squire Carter was amazed.

"Can he row?" he asked.

"Yes, a little."

"But he beat you?"

"I will tell you how it was, father," said Conrad, who had decided upon his story. "I was well ahead till we got halfway back, when I got a terrible pain in my arm. I must have strained it, I think. Of course I couldn't do anything after that, and Andy, who was next to me, went in and won."

Squire Carter never thought of doubting Conrad's story. His pride extended to his family and all connected with him, and he felt satisfied that Conrad was the best rower in the village.

"Where did the Grant boy learn to row?" he asked.

"I heard him tell Mr. Gale that he learned at the academy."

"You don't think he is equal to you?"

"Of course he isn't. I am miles ahead of him."

"It was very unfortunate that your arm gave out. You had better speak to your mother, and she will put some ointment on it."

"I will," said Conrad cunningly. "I would rather have had any boy beat me than that upstart, Andy Grant. He will put on no end of airs. Besides, I shall miss the money."

"That, at any rate, I can make up to you. Here are two five-dollar bills."

"Thank you, father," said Conrad as, with much satisfaction, he pocketed the bills. "It was lucky I thought about the strain," he said to himself. "All the same, it is awfully humiliating to be beaten by that beggar."

"How do you think Conrad accounts for his defeat, Andy?" said Valentine the next day.

"I can't tell."

"He says he strained the muscles of his arm."

Andy smiled.

"If it will make him feel any better, I have no objection to that explanation."

"His father has given him ten dollars, so he will not lose any money. But he won't get any of the boys to believe his story."

"The money is very acceptable to me," said Andy. "If I had lost, my father couldn't have made it up to me."

At five o'clock, on his way to the post office, Andy met Mr. Gale.

Walter Gale was a young man of about twenty-five. He had a pleasant face, and his manner was genial. He had a strong sympathy with boys, and he was a favorite with them.

"Well, Andrew," he said, "have you recovered from your exertions in the boat race?"

"Oh, yes. I am used to rowing and felt very little fatigue."

"I hear that Conrad is very much mortified by his defeat."

"I believe he is. He felt sure of winning."

"And he would have done so if you had remained out of the list."

"He told Valentine Burns that he strained the muscles of his arm, and that this defeated him."

"I should think better of him if he would acknowledge that he was fairly beaten. Are you at leisure this evening?"

"Yes, sir."

"Then call upon me at the hotel. I shall be glad to know you better."

This invitation Andy was very glad to accept. He was drawn to the young man and felt that he was likely to prove a sincere friend.

At seven o'clock he left the farmhouse and on arriving at the hotel found Mr. Gale sitting on the piazza.

"I was looking for you," said the young man. "Come up to my room."

He led the way to a front corner apartment on the second floor. It was the best room in the hotel, and he had furnished it in the most comfortable and attractive manner. Pictures hung on the walls, and there was a bookcase containing a goodly array of volumes.

Mr. Gale sits on the piazza at a fine hotel.

"What a pleasant room!" exclaimed Andy.

"Yes, I have tried to make myself comfortable. What I lack most is society."

"I wonder that you are content to live in the country. Are you not accustomed to the city?"

"Yes, but I had a severe sickness in the spring, and the doctors recommended me to absent myself for a time from the excitement of the town and take up my residence in the country."

"Didn't that interfere with your business?"

Walter Gale smiled.

"Fortunately, or unfortunately," he answered, "I have no business. Until two years ago I was employed in an insurance office in the city. The death of an uncle has made me financially independent, so that I had leisure to be sick."

"You look in good health now."

"Yes, but I have a nervous temperament and am obliged to be careful. Now tell me about yourself. You have been for some time at Penhurst Academy?"

"Yes, for two years."

"Do you go back there?"

"No. My father has met with serious losses and can no longer afford to send me. I must stay at home and help him."

"And this is a disappointment to you?"

"Yes. I was expecting to go to college in a few months."

"I believe your father is a farmer?"

"Yes."

"Do you expect to assist him on the farm?"

"Till I can get something to do. I shall try to get some business situation. Business pays better than farming."

"I suppose you are a good Latin and Greek scholar?"

"Yes, that is, I like the languages and stood high in my classes."

"My own education is limited. Though I am rich now, I was a poor boy. At sixteen I had made some progress in Latin and commenced Greek until my father's failure obliged me to seek employment. The uncle who has now made me rich would do nothing for me, so I left school half educated."

"You would be able to make up deficiencies now," suggested Andy.

"That is what I have been thinking of, if I can get a satisfactory teacher."

"I don't think you can find a classical teacher in Arden."

"I know of one, if he would be willing to undertake the task."

"Who is it?" asked Andy puzzled.

"Andrew Grant," answered this young man with a smile.

"Do you mean me?" asked Andy with a wondering face.

"Certainly. You are fresh from school, and I am sure you would be competent to teach me."

"But I am only a boy."

"Age has nothing to do with a teacher's qualifications, except as to discipline. You wouldn't find me a very advanced pupil. I had read one book in Caesar when I was compelled to leave school, and had begun to translate Greek a little. Now the question is, are you willing to teach me?"

"If you think I am competent, Mr. Gale."

"I don't doubt that. We will begin, if you like, next Monday. Perhaps, in order to avoid village gossip, it will be well to pass yourself off as my private secretary. Indeed, I will employ you a little in that way also."

"I shall be very glad to serve you in any way."

"Then come tomorrow morning at nine and remain with me till twelve. Now about the compensation."

"Fix that to suit yourself, Mr. Gale. I am almost ashamed to ask anything."

"The laborer is worthy of his hire, Andy. Suppose I pay you six dollars a week to begin with?"

"The money will be very acceptable, but I am afraid you will be overpaying me."

"I will risk it. On the whole, I will call it nine dollars a week, and we will spend the afternoon together also. I will send to the city for a boat, and you shall give me lessons in rowing."

Andy's eyes sparkled. Nothing would please him more, and the prospect of earning nine dollars a week made him feel like a millionaire.

CHAPTER VII

AN ENCOUNTER WITH A TRAMP

It is hardly necessary to say that Andy's parents were equally surprised and pleased at his new engagement.

"You will like that better than working on the farm, I expect, Andy?" said Sterling Grant.

"Yes, father. I am willing to work, but I don't feel much interest in farming."

"It is hard work and poor pay, Andy, but I like it. I was brought up to it when a boy, and there is nothing else I can do."

"Andy is already beginning to get some advantage from his education," said Mrs. Grant.

Andy reported for duty, and during the first morning made up his mind that he should enjoy his new employment. Mr. Gale really desired to acquire a knowledge of Latin and Greek, and he worked faithfully.

To Andy it was like a review of his own studies, and he experienced a satisfaction in the rapid progress of his pupil.

He felt quite at home with Mr. Gale, though their acquaintance had been so brief. When twelve o'clock came he was really sorry.

"What time shall I come over this afternoon, Mr. Gale?" he asked.

"At two o'clock. Can you borrow your friend Valentine's boat? I have sent for one, but it may be several days before it arrives."

"Oh, yes. I am sure Val will let me have it. He is a very good-natured boy."

"I will be glad to pay for its use."

"I don't think he'd accept anything."

"Then I will make him a present."

Before he returned to the hotel, Andy saw Valentine and obtained the loan of his boat.

At three o'clock Mr. Gale and Andy started from the boathouse, and again Andy became a teacher.

The young man was a good rower, but Andy was able to give him some points. Sometimes they sat idle and let the boat float at will.

About four o'clock Conrad came down for his usual afternoon row. He was surprised and not altogether pleased at meeting Andy and his companion.

"Why are you not hoeing potatoes?" he asked.

"I've got a vacation," answered Andy with a smile.

"Are you out for a row?" inquired Mr. Gale pleasantly.

"Yes," answered Conrad sullenly.

Though Walter Gale had nothing to do with his defeat, he could not quite forgive him for awarding the prize to Andy. He felt mortified whenever he thought of it and wished Mr. Gale to understand that he was not inferior to Andy.

"I was unlucky the other day," he said. "I strained my muscles or I would not have been beaten."

"That was lucky for me, then," said Andy good-naturedly.

"I didn't care so much for the money, but if I had been in my usual form I should have gained the prize."

"Then you wouldn't object to a second race?" said Walter Gale quietly.

"What do you mean?"

"If you would like to try it again over the same course, I will put up five dollars."

Conrad hesitated.

He would not object to winning five dollars. Indeed, he wished very much to have that sum, but he was not quite so sure that he could beat Andy as he claimed to be.

Should Andy win again, he would be obliged to concede his superiority.

"No," he said after a pause, "I don't think I care to race again."

"Then I will make you another offer, but not so good a one. I row a little myself -- indeed, Andy is training me so that I hope soon to row better. If you will row against me, I will pay you two dollars. That will be the prize."

"But suppose you win?"

"Then I keep the two dollars myself. It will cost you nothing."

"I'll row," said Conrad eagerly.

"Very well. We will appoint Andy umpire, or referee, whatever you call it."

Conrad was not altogether pleased with this selection, but he waived his objections and the race was rowed, Andy giving the signal.

Conrad won by a dozen lengths, Mr. Gale making a very good second.

"You have won, Conrad," said the young man good-naturedly. "Here is the prize."

Conrad pocketed the bill with a good deal of satisfaction.

"I will row you any day," he said.

Walter Gale shook his head.

"I must wait till I have improved," he said, "or you will beat me every time."

Conrad would much prefer to have beaten Andy, but the two dollars gave him not a little satisfaction.

"Mr. Gale must be rich," he reflected. "I wish I could get in with him."

"As Andy has to work on the farm," he said, "I shall be glad to go out with you any afternoon."

"Thank you, but I have made an arrangement with Andy that will save him from the necessity of farm work."

Conrad opened his eyes in surprise.

Later in the evening, when he met Andy at the village store, he asked, "How much does Mr. Gale pay you for going with him?"

"The arrangement is private, Conrad, or I would tell you."

"How much are you with him?"

"I go to the hotel at nine o'clock in the morning."

"What do you do then?"

"He calls me his private secretary."

"Do you get as much as three dollars a week?"

"I am sorry, I can't tell you."

"Oh, well, if it is such a profound secret. You seem to have got in with him."

"He treats me very kindly."

"Is he rich?"

"I don't know, but I presume he is."

"I don't see what keeps him in such a dull hole as Arden, when he could live in the city and be in the midst of things."

"At any rate, it is lucky for me that he chooses to stay here."

"What on earth does he want of a private secretary?" demanded Conrad.

"Perhaps you had better ask him."

"Probably he only hires you out of pity."

"I won't trouble myself about his motives, as long as he appears to like having me with him."

Several days passed. The mornings were spent in study, the afternoons on the pond.

There had been no change in the program, so that Andy was surprised when, one morning, Mr. Gale said, "We will omit our lessons this morning. I am going to send you to Benton on an errand."

"Very well, sir."

"I have an account with the bank and will send a check by you to be cashed."

"All right, sir."

"I will engage a top buggy for you at the hotel stable. I suppose you are used to driving?"

"Oh, yes, sir."

"And I suppose you know the way to Benton?"

"I have been there a good many times."

"Then there will be no trouble."

"When do you want me to start?"

"At eleven o'clock. That would get you home late for lunch. You may, therefore, stop and dine at the hotel in Benton."

This would make it a day's excursion. Andy liked driving, and the visit to Benton would be a pleasure to him.

"I will run home and tell mother I shall not be back for lunch," he said.

"Very well. Be back here at eleven o'clock."

"All right, sir."

When Andy reached the hotel on his return he found the buggy ready. Harnessed to it was the best horse in the hotel stable.

"A pleasant journey to you!" said Walter Gale, smiling at Andy from the piazza.

"Thank you, sir."

Andy drove off at good speed. It was a bright, clear morning. The air was invigorating, and his spirits rose.

He reflected upon his good luck in having found such a friend as Walter Gale. He had been unfortunate, to be sure, in being compelled to leave school, but the hardship was very much mitigated by Mr. Gale's friendship.

He had gone two-thirds of the way when he overtook a man whose bloated look and shabby clothing proclaimed him to belong to the large class of tramps whose business seems to be to roam through the country in quest of plunder.

The man looked up as Andy reached him.

"I say, boy," he called out, "give me a lift, won't you?"

Andy was kind-hearted, but he was repelled by the unsavory look of the man who asked him this favor. He felt that it would be very unpleasant to have such a man sitting beside him in the buggy.

"I think you must excuse me," he said.

"What for?" asked the man with a scowl. "Are you too proud to take in a poor man?"

"I don't object to you being poor," answered Andy, "but you look as if you had been drinking."

The man replied by an oath, and, bending over, he picked up a good-sized stone and flung it at the young driver. Fortunately his condition made his aim unsteady, and the stone flew wide of the mark.

Andy whipped up the horse and was soon out of danger.

CHAPTER VIII

A MOMENT OF DANGER

Andy did not examine the check till he reached the bank in Benton. Then, glancing at it before he presented it to the paying teller, he found that it was for one hundred and twenty-five dollars.

"How will you have it?" asked the teller.

"Twenty-five dollars in small bills; the rest in fives and tens," answered Andy as instructed by Mr. Gale.

The bills were counted out and placed in his hands. To Andy they seemed a large sum of money, and, indeed, the roll was big enough to convey that impression.

As he left the bank he saw the familiar but not welcome face of the tramp who had stopped him glued against the pane. He had attended to some errands before going to the bank, which allowed the fellow time to reach it in time to watch him.

"I wonder if he saw me putting away the bills?" thought Andy.

However, in a town like Benton, there was little chance of robbery.

The tramp looked at him with evil significance as he left the bank.

"Give me a dollar," he said.

"I can't," answered Andy.

"I saw you with a big roll of bills."

"They are not mine."

"Give me enough to buy lunch, then," growled the tramp.

"Why should I give you anything? You threw a stone at me on the road."

The tramp turned away muttering, and the glance with which he eyed Andy was far from friendly.

As directed, Andy went over to the hotel and got lunch. He took the opportunity to dispose of the bills, putting all the large ones in his inside vest pocket. The small bills he distributed among his other pockets.

Andy started for home at two o'clock. He felt some responsibility, remembering that he had a considerable sum of money with him.

This made him anxious, and he felt that he should be glad to get home safe and deliver his funds to Mr. Gale. Probably he would not have thought of danger if he had not met the tramp on his way over.

The road for the most part was clear and open, but there was one portion, perhaps a third of a mile in length, bordered by trees and underbrush. It was so short, however, that it would be soon passed over.

But about the middle of it a man sprang from the side of the road and seized the horse by the bridle. It did not require a second look to satisfy Andy that it was the tramp.

The crisis had come! Andy's heart was in his mouth. He was a brave boy, but it might well make even an older person nervous to be stopped by an ill-looking tramp, who was without doubt a criminal.

"Let go that bridle!" called Andy in a tone which, in spite of his nervousness, was clear and resolute.

"So I will when I have got what I want," answered the tramp.

"What do you want?"

"Look at me and you can tell what I want."

"I presume you want money, but I have none to give you."

"You are lying. You have plenty of money about your clothes."

"I said I had no money to give you."

"Didn't I see you get a roll of bills at the bank?"

"Very likely you did, but what about that?"

"I want some of them. I won't take all, but I am a poor man, and I need them more than the man you are taking them to."

"Whom do you think I am taking them to?"

"Squire Carter. He is the only man in Arden who keeps so much money in the bank."

"You are mistaken; the money is not his."

"Whose, then?"

"I don't feel called upon to tell you."

"Well, that's neither here nor there. I want some of it. I'll be content with half, whoever owns it."

"You won't get any. Let go the horse, or I'll run you down."

"You're a smart kid, but you are no match for me. I don't scare worth a cent."

Listen to me," said Andy. "If you should succeed in robbing me, you would be caught and sent to jail. How will that suit you?"

"It wouldn't be the first time I've been in jail. I'd just as soon be there as to tramp around without a cent of money."

—

Andy encounters a tramp.

Andy was not surprised to hear that he had to deal with an ex-convict. He understood that this man was a desperate character. He saw that he was a strong, powerful man, in the full vigor of life.

Any contest between them would be most unequal. He was but sixteen and the tramp was near forty. What could he do?

"I'll tell you what I'll do," he said, willing to try an experiment. "I've got two dollars of my own. I'll give you that if you'll let go my horse's bridle and give me no more trouble."

The tramp laughed mockingly.

"Do you take me for a fool?" he asked.

"Why?"

"Do you think I will be satisfied with two dollars, when you have a hundred in your pocket? Two dollars wouldn't last me a day."

"I have nothing to do with that. It is all I mean to give you."

"Then I shall have to help myself."

His cool impudence made Andy angry, and he brought down the whip forcibly on the horse's back.

Naturally the animal started, and nearly tore himself from the grasp of the tramp.

"So that is your game," said the fellow between his closed teeth. "If you try that again I'll pull you out of the buggy and give you such a beating as you never had before."

Andy remained cool and self-possessed. To carry out his threat the tramp would have to let go of the bridle, and in that case Andy determined to put his horse to his paces.

The tramp relaxed his hold and the horse stood stock-still, finding his attempt to get away futile.

"Well," said the tramp, "you didn't make much by that move, did you?"

"Did you make any more?"

"By Jove! You're a cool kid. But, after all, you're only a kid. Now, do as I tell you."

"What is that?"

"Put your hand in your pocket and take out fifty dollars. You've got that much, haven't you?"

"Yes."

"That's right. Speak the truth. You may have more, but fifty'll do me."

"Do you expect me to give you fifty dollars?"

"Yes, I do."

"I don't mean to do it."

Andy had satisfied himself that the tramp had no weapon, and this encouraged him. He could not hold the horse and attack him at one and the same time, but with a revolver he would have been at his mercy.

Besides, Andy's ears were keen, and he thought he heard the sound of wheels behind him. The tramp's attention was too much occupied, and perhaps his hearing was too dull to catch the sounds, as yet faint.

Thus it was that the other team was almost upon them before the tramp was aware of it. The newcomer was Saul Wheelock, a blacksmith and a strong, powerful man, fully six feet in height and with muscles of steel.

He had seen the buggy standing still on the highway, and he could not understand the cause until he got near enough to see the tramp at the horse's head.

He sprang from the wagon he was driving, and before the vagabond was fully sensible of his danger, he had him by the coat collar.

"What are you about?" he demanded, giving him a rough shake.

The tramp, turning, found he was in the hands of a man whom he was compelled to respect. He cared nothing for rank or learning, but physical force held him in awe.

He stood mute, unprepared with an excuse.

"Why, it's you, Andy!" said the blacksmith. "Why did this rascal stop you?"

"He wants me to give him money. I've just been to the bank in Benton to draw out some for Mr. Gale at the hotel."

"Why, you scoundrel!" exclaimed the indignant blacksmith, shaking the tramp till his teeth chattered. "So you're a thief, are you?"

"Let me go!" whined the tramp. "I haven't taken anything. I'm a poor, unfortunate man. If I could get any work to do I wouldn't have been driven to this."

"No doubt you're a church member," said the blacksmith in a sarcastic tone.

"Let me go! I'll promise to lead a good life. This young man says he'll give me two dollars. I'll take it and go."

"Don't give him a cent, Andy. You can go, but I'll give you something to remember me by."

He gave the tramp a vigorous kick that nearly prostrated him, and then, getting into his wagon, said, "I'll keep along with you, Andy. I don't think you'll have any more trouble."

The tramp slunk into the woods, baffled and disappointed. If looks could have annihilated the sturdy blacksmith, his span of life would have been brief.

CHAPTER IX

CONRAD'S SCHEME

When Andy told Mr. Gale the story of his adventures on the trip to Benton, he received cordial congratulations on his courage.

"You have shown a great deal of pluck, Andy," he said. "The next time you have occasion to go over to the bank for me I will accompany you. Now, if you are not too tired, I want you to go down to the pond. I have something to show you."

They walked side by side till they reached the pond.

Andy's curiosity was not specially excited. He talked with Mr. Gale on different topics and had hardly time to consider what it was he was to see. But when he reached the boathouse he saw floating at the small pier an elegant rowboat built of cedar and much handsomer than either Conrad's or Valentine's.

"Oh, what a beauty!" he exclaimed.

"Yes," said Mr. Gale quietly. "You will have quite the best boat on the pond."

"I?" exclaimed Andy in surprise.

"Yes, for the boat is yours."

"But I don't understand," stammered Andy.

"It is plain enough," said Walter Gale with a pleasant smile. "The boat is yours. I give it to you."

"How can I thank you?" exclaimed Andy, grasping his friend's hand. "I can't believe that this beautiful boat is mine."

"You will realize it after a while. Let me tell you how I got it. It was built for a rich young man in New York, one of the Four Hundred, I believe, but as he received an unexpected invitation to go abroad for two years, he authorized the builder to sell it for him at a considerable reduction from the price he paid. So it happens that I was able to secure it for you. Now let us go out for a row. It will be the trial trip."

Fifteen minutes later Conrad got into his boat and started out. It was not long before his eyes were attracted to the new boat.

He could see at once, for he was a judge, that it was far more elegant and costly than his own, and he was seized by a pang of envy. His own boat seemed to him quite inferior, though but a short time before he had regarded it with pride.

He was curious to see the craft and pulled up to it.

46

"That is a fine boat you have there, Mr. Gale," he said.

"So I think," returned the young man. "I feel quite satisfied with it."

"When did it come down?"

"I only received it this morning."

"How much did it cost?" asked Conrad, who was not troubled by bashfulness.

"A small fortune," answered Walter Gale with a smile. "I am afraid I must decline to give the exact figures."

"I asked because I may ask my father to buy me one like it."

Conrad was perfectly well aware that such a request would be promptly denied. Squire Carter was not disposed to be extravagant, and he had even hesitated for some time before incurring the outlay required for Conrad's present boat.

The new boat was so elegant, so graceful, and so thoroughly finished in every part, that Conrad could not help coveting it. He was not very much to be blamed, for it was one that would captivate the fancy of any boy who was fond of the water.

"I should like to try the boat some time, Mr. Gale," he said.

"If the owner is willing, I am," returned the young man.

"The owner? Why, doesn't it belong to you?" asked Conrad in surprise.

"No, it belongs to Andy."

"That boat belongs to Andy Grant?" exclaimed Conrad with an incredulous frown.

"Yes. I have given it to him. You will have to ask his permission."

"I shall be glad to have you try it," said Andy pleasantly.

"Thank you, but I don't think I care for it," replied Conrad coldly.

He felt a pang of mortification to think that the farmer's son should have a boat so much superior to his own.

"If you change your mind, let me know," said Andy.

"Conrad is jealous," remarked Walter Gale. "He doesn't like to have you own a boat that is superior to his."

"I think you are right, Mr. Gale. If the case were reversed I would not mind."

"Because you are not disposed to be envious or jealous."

When Conrad returned home there was a cloud upon his brow. It was easy for anyone to see that he was in bad humor.

47

"What is the matter, Conrad?" asked his father. "You look as if you had lost your best friend."

"I hate Andy Grant," exploded Conrad, his eyes flashing with anger.

"Why, what has Andy done now? You haven't had a fight, have you?"

"No. I wouldn't demean myself by fighting with him."

"What is it, then?"

"He is always doing something to annoy me."

"I am still in the dark."

"He has got a new boat, far handsomer than mine. I shouldn't wonder if it cost twice as much."

Squire Carter was surprised.

"Where did he get it?" he inquired.

"It was a present from Mr. Gale, the young man at the hotel."

"He must like young Grant very much?"

"It is ridiculous that a poor boy should own such a boat."

"I don't see how we can help it," said the squire philosophically.

He did not take the superiority of Andy's boat so much to heart as his son.

"I'll tell you how you can make it right, father."

"How?"

"By buying me a boat as good or better than the new one."

"Why should I buy you another boat? The one you have is only six months old, and it cost me a pretty penny, I assure you."

"That may be, but I shall not feel any more satisfaction in it, now that Andy has a better one."

"All this is foolish, my son."

"Then you won't buy me a new boat?"

"Most certainly I won't," said the squire firmly.

Conrad's countenance fell, but another idea came to him.

"Suppose Andy is willing to exchange with me something for the boat?"

"You say the boat is a fine one?"

"Elegant."

"You may offer him ten dollars."

"Won't you say fifteen, father? I assure you it is worth much more than that difference."

"You can offer him ten dollars, and see what he has to say to it."

Conrad managed to see Andy the next day and made him the offer.

"Do you think I would part with Mr. Gale's gift?" said Andy indignantly.

"He wouldn't care, and ten dollars is a good deal of money," said Conrad insinuatingly.

"If you offered me fifty dollars I would say the same. I am not particularly in want of money."

"I suppose you say that because you are earning three dollars a week."

"Who told you how much Mr. Gale paid me?" asked Andy smiling.

"Then he does get three dollars a week," reflected Conrad.

He redoubled his entreaties, but Andy refused firmly.

Half an hour later Conrad met on the street a shabby figure with whom we are already acquainted. It was the tramp who figured in an encounter with Andy when on his way to Benton.

"Young gentleman," said the tramp with a whine, "you look rich and generous. Can't you spare a poor man a trifle?"

"You look as if you drank," replied Conrad with brutal frankness. "Your nose is red."

"That's owing to a skin disease. I have belonged to the Temperance Society for five years."

"Humph! You don't look like it. Why don't you work?"

"Because I can find nothing to do."

Here a contemptible suggestion offered itself to Conrad.

"If you will do something for me, and keep mum, I'll give you two dollars."

"I'll do it if it isn't too hard."

"Then I'll tell you what it is. There's a boat on the pond that belongs to an enemy of mine. He is always crowing over me. Now, if you'll manage this evening to set it on fire, I'll give you two dollars."

"How shall I set it on fire? With a match?"

"No. I'll supply you with some shavings, a few pieces of board, and some pitch. There won't be any trouble about it."

"Who owns the boat?"

Conrad described Andy.

"That's the boy who -- but never mind! I'll do it."

49

Once convinced that in this way he could get revenge on the boy who had humiliated and gotten the best of him, the tramp was only too willing to help Conrad in his scheme.

When Conrad went home at nine o'clock, after supplying the tramp with combustibles, he said to himself, "There won't be much left of Andy's boat in the morning."

CHAPTER X

THE TRAMP'S MISTAKE

Conrad went to bed with the comfortable conviction that before morning Andy's beautiful boat would be ruined. I am sorry to say that the meanness of the act which he had instigated did not strike him.

Whatever feeling he had was of exultation at the injury done to his enemy, as he persisted in regarding Andy.

It did seem a pity that such an elegant boat should be destroyed. If Andy would only have agreed to exchange for ten -- even fifteen -- dollars to boot, this would have been avoided.

"He was a fool not to accept," soliloquized Conrad. "He will regret it when he sees what has happened."

He got up at the usual hour and took breakfast. Every time the bell rang he thought it might be someone to bring him the desired news.

Just after supper that evening Andy met his friend, Valentine, and told him of the beautiful gift he had received.

"Come down and look at it, Val," he said. "It is elegant."

Valentine's curiosity was excited, and he at once accepted the invitation.

He uttered an exclamation of surprise when he saw the new boat.

"It is a little beauty!" he said. "It is far ahead of Conrad's or of mine."

"Conrad wants to exchange. He offered me ten dollars to boot."

"You wouldn't think of accepting?"

"No, it is worth much more than that. Besides, it is Mr. Gale's gift, and even if he had offered fifty dollars I should still refuse."

"And you would do right, too. But are you going to leave it out all night?"

"I shall have to. I have no boathouse to put it in."

"There is room in my boathouse for two boats," said Valentine. "I will help you put it inside."

"Thank you, Val. I will be glad to pay you rent for the use of the place."

"I don't want any money, Andy; I will do it out of friendship."

"Thank you, but you mustn't forget that I am quite able to pay."

"That's true, and I am glad of it; but, all the same, I don't want any money."

"I wonder Conrad doesn't have a boathouse."

"He tells me his father has promised him one. He has not yet decided upon a location."

The two boys got into Andy's boat and rowed it a few rods till they reached the boathouse. There was no difficulty in putting it away. The boathouse was a double, and there was room for two boats.

"I will have another key made, Andy, so that you can get at your boat when I am not with you."

"All right! That will be very nice."

"How do you like Mr. Gale?"

"Tiptop. I was very fortunate to fall in with him. It will be a great loss to me when he goes away."

"Is he thinking of going soon?"

"I don't think so -- I hope not."

It was later in the evening when the tramp went down to the pond, provided with the shavings and other combustibles which Conrad had provided.

Conrad, after meeting him, had gone home at once. He thought it more prudent, in view of the plot in which he was engaged, to avoid suspicion by not being seen in company with the tramp.

"Give me the two dollars now," said the tramp when the fuel was handed him.

"Do you think I am a fool?" answered Conrad sharply. "If I should do that, you would go off and not do the work."

"I'll do the work fast enough. I want to get even with that young rascal."

"What! Do you know him?"

"I have met him," answered the tramp evasively. "He played me a mean trick, and I want to get even with him."

"What sort of a trick was it?"

"I will tell you some other time -- I haven't time now. I wish I had a hatchet."

"What for?"

"Then, if the fire didn't spoil the boat, I'd hack it up."

"I think I can get you a hatchet, but you must not leave it on the bank, for my father's initial, 'C,' is on it."

"All right. I'll be careful."

52

The hatchet was delivered to the tramp a little later.

About eight o'clock the tramp went down to the lake and looked for Andy's boat.

There was but one in sight -- Conrad's -- but the tramp never doubted that this was the one he was to destroy. He waited till half-past eight, when he considered it dark enough for his purpose.

He carefully laid the shavings in one end of the boat, covered them over with pieces of board which, with the help of the hatchet, he split into smaller pieces, and then set them on fire.

The flames blazed fiercely and did considerable damage to the boat, not ruining it, however. But to finish the work he used the hatchet and hacked vigorously at the woodwork till it was mutilated and its usefulness and beauty spoiled.

The tramp contemplated this work with satisfaction.

"I've done the job pretty well," he chuckled to himself. "I'd like to be lookin' on when the boy sees it."

Now that he had done the job he wanted his pay. Conrad had agreed to meet him at an old ruined barn not far from his house at eight o'clock in the morning.

"It won't do to call for me earlier," he said, "for it might excite suspicion."

From the breakfast table Conrad directed his steps to the barn.

The tramp was sitting outside, smoking a pipe.

"I've been waiting for you," he said. "I haven't had any breakfast."

"Did you do the job?"

"Did I? Well, I reckon. That boat ain't no good any more."

"Do you think anyone saw you do it?"

"No, it was pretty dark, and there wasn't no one round. It may have been found out by now. Give me the two dollars and I'll be off."

"You are sure you did the job? You are not deceiving me?"

"No, I'm not. You can go and see for yourself."

This, however, did not seem prudent. Conrad wished someone else to discover the ruined boat.

After all, there was no reason to doubt the tramp's word. His avowed hostility to Andy made it quite certain that he had done his work.

"Here's the money," he said.

"And here's the hatchet."

"I wish it was back in the tool house where it belongs," thought Conrad. "However, I'll manage to get it back without anyone seeing me."

He decided to return to the barn at once, carrying the hatchet with him. He was not to do it without observation. Just before he reached the barn he met John Larkin.

"What are you doing with the hatchet, Conrad?"

"Oh, I have been using it in the pasture."

"I didn't know but you were going to imitate George Washington and cut down a cherry tree."

"Perhaps I have," said Conrad with a smile.

He felt in good humor for his plan had been carried out. He was aching to see just how badly Andy's boat was injured, and as there was no school, it being Saturday, he proposed to John Larkin to go down to the pond.

"Suppose we have a row, John," he said. "We'll take a trip across the pond."

"All right."

They were perhaps thirty rods from the pond when they met Jimmy Morris, coming from it. He seemed excited. He had been running and was breathless.

"What's the matter, Jimmy?" asked John Larkin.

Jimmy looked toward Conrad, who naturally guessed the cause of his excitement.

"Oh, Conrad," he said. "It is such a pity! I am so sorry for you!"

"Why are you sorry for me?" demanded Conrad sharply.

Because your boat is ruined. It is all hacked up and has been set on fire."

"My boat! You mean Andy Grant's?"

"No, I don't. Come and see for yourself."

CHAPTER XI

CONRAD'S DISAPPOINTMENT

With his mind in a whirl and still believing that it was Andy's boat which had been injured instead of his own, Conrad pushed on rapidly toward the pond. Yet he had an instinctive fear that his informant might be correct.

When he reached the point where his boat had been moored, he used his eyes eagerly.

It was all true! His boat -- his beautiful boat -- with which he had been perfectly satisfied till Andy received a better, was scorched and hacked up till it was clear he could never use it again, and Andy's boat was not visible anywhere. Tears of rage filled Conrad's eyes.

"It is a terrible mistake!" he said.

"Mistake! What do you mean?" asked John Larkin.

Conrad reflected that his words were betraying him.

"I don't know what I am saying," he replied vaguely. "Yes, I do. I believe Andy Grant did this."

"Andy Grant!" repeated Jimmy Morris. "Why should he injure your boat?"

"Because he hates me."

"Andy isn't that kind of a boy. Besides, he has a newer and much handsomer boat himself."

There it was! That was what stung Conrad. His boat was second to Andy's.

As the three boys stood on the bank, a small boy named Peter Hill came up. He lived in the house nearest the boats.

"Did you see anyone near the boat, Peter?" asked John Larkin.

"Yes, I seed a big tramp in de boat. He set it on fire."

"That explains it, Conrad!" exclaimed Jimmy Morris. "I saw the tramp myself in the village."

"Pooh!" said Conrad. "I don't believe it."

"But I seed him burnin' de boat!" persisted little Peter.

"Then why didn't you tell somebody?"

"All de folks was away, and I didn't dare to go near it. He had a hatchet, too."

"I say, Conrad, let us hunt for the tramp and, if we find him, have him arrested."

For obvious reasons this proposal of John Larkin did not meet Conrad's approval. He was afraid of what the tramp would tell.

"I'll ask my father what to do," he replied evasively. "The mischief is done and there is no help for it."

Conrad was already looking more cheerful. An idea had come to him.

Now that the boat was destroyed, his father might be willing to buy him another, and, if so, he might be persuaded to buy one as good as Andy's, perhaps better. He turned to go home, and let the boys know that he did not care for company.

On the way, not far from his own house, he encountered the tramp. At the sight of this man, whose stupid blunder had cost him his boat, his eyes blazed with anger.

But this the tramp did not see. He slouched up to his young employer saying, with a cunning grin, "Well, did you see it?"

"Did I see it?" repeated Conrad boiling over with fury. "Yes, I did."

"I did it pretty well, didn't I? I guess the boat isn't good for much now."

"You stupid fool!" blazed out Conrad. "It is my boat that you ruined. I have a great mind to have you arrested!"

"Your boat? It was the boat you pointed out to me."

"No, it wasn't. It was my own boat."

"Then where was the other boat? I didn't see but one."

"I don't know, but you might have had sense enough to know that you'd got the wrong boat."

The tramp's hopes fell. He had intended to ask for another dollar from Conrad, but he saw now that there was no chance whatsoever of his obtaining it.

"You'd better get out of town as soon as you can," said Conrad roughly.

"Why should I?" demanded the tramp sullenly.

"Because you were seen destroying the boat."

"Who saw me?"

"A small boy who lives at the next house. You might be arrested."

"If I am, I'll tell the truth. I'll tell who put me up to it."

"And I'll deny it. Do you think anyone would believe your word against mine, especially as it was my boat that was ruined?"

The tramp saw the logic of this remark and walked away. He was seen no more in the village.

"Now I'll tackle father," thought Conrad.

He directed his steps homeward and informed the squire of what had happened.

His father frowned and looked displeased.

"If you are not smart enough to take care of your boat," he said coldly, "you will have to suffer the consequences."

"But I don't see how I am to blame?"

"Have you any idea who did the mischief?"

"Perhaps Andy Grant did -- he doesn't like me."

"I don't think that very probable. You can charge him with it if you think best. But I thought you told me he had a new boat of his own?"

"So he has -- a perfect beauty! It is ever so much better than mine. I wish -- "

"Well, what do you wish?"

"That you would buy me one like his."

"Well, I like that. After losing your boat through your own carelessness, you want me to invest a large sum in another."

"Must I go without one, then?" asked Conrad in dismay.

"It looks that way."

Conrad resorted to earnest entreaties. He was willing, now, to accept any sort of boat, for he was fond of rowing; but Squire Carter had just heard unfavorable reports from his broker about a speculation he had entered into, and he was inflexible.

"What a fool I was!" reflected Conrad bitterly. "My boat was a good one, even if it wasn't as fine as Andy's, and now I have none. I shall have to borrow his or Valentine's when I want to go out rowing."

Later in the day he met Andy.

Andy had heard of Conrad's loss and was full of sympathy.

"Conrad," he said, "it's a shame about your boat being destroyed."

"Yes, it is pretty hard."

"The boys say a tramp did the mischief."

"I think it very likely. There was a tramp about town yesterday. I saw him myself."

"What could have been his object? Ruining the boat would not benefit him."

"It might have been out of revenge. He asked me for a quarter and I wouldn't give it to him."

This explanation occurred to Conrad on the spur of the moment.

"Can't you have him arrested?"

"He is probably out of town by this time."

"I suppose you will have a new boat?"

"Yes, after a while."

"I will lend you mine any time you wish."

"Thank you," said Conrad, but he spoke coldly and ungraciously.

It seemed to him humiliating to receive any favors from a poor boy like Andy Grant.

Two weeks later, when Andy went over to the hotel, as usual, to meet his employer and pupil, Mr. Gale said, "I have some news for you."

"I hope it is good news."

"I don't know that you will consider it so. I shall have to leave you for a time."

Andy's face fell. This certainly was bad news.

"I have received a letter this morning," continued Walter Gale, "from an uncle living in the interior of Pennsylvania. He is not an old man -- I don't think he is much over fifty -- but he writes me that he is near his end. The doctor says he may live three months, certainly not over six. He has always been a bachelor, and I believe he owns coal mines of considerable value. I was always a favorite of his, and now that he is so sick he wants me to go out and be with him in the closing weeks of his life."

"I suppose you will go?" said Andy, and he looked very sober.

"I think it is my duty -- don't you?"

"Yes, I suppose it is your duty."

Andy began to think what he should do. He had had an easy and profitable engagement with Mr. Gale, but this would now be over, and he would have to go back to farm work or try to get a place in the village store.

The latter would yield him only two dollars and a half a week, which seemed to him very small compared with what he now received.

"I shall miss you very much, Mr. Gale," he said.

"I hope you will. I shall certainly miss you."

"It will seem very dull going to work on the farm after my pleasant days with you."

"You won't need to go to work on the farm, unless you choose to do so."

"But I must earn something. I cannot be idle."

"Oh, I forgot to tell you what arrangements I propose to make for you."

Andy looked up eagerly.

CHAPTER XII

SOMETHING UNEXPECTED

"Our separation will only be temporary," continued Mr. Gale, "but as I do not wish to leave you unprovided for during my absence, I shall allow you five dollars a week while I am away."

Andy brightened up.

"How kind you are, Mr. Gale!" he said. "I don't think you ought to do this."

Walter Gale smiled.

"I can very well afford it," he said. "So we will regard the matter as settled."

"How soon must you go?"

"I shall start tomorrow -- my preparations will be easily made. How would you like to go to New York to see me off?"

"I should be delighted," answered Andy. "I have only been to New York twice in my life."

"Then you will enjoy the day. You can take the afternoon train home."

At the farm, Mr. and Mrs. Grant heard with regret of Mr. Gale's departure, but they were pleased to hear that Andy would be in receipt of an income.

"How will you fill up your time, Andy?" asked his father.

"I have my books and will keep up my Latin and Greek. I will pay you four dollars a week, and you can hire a boy for that to help you. I think I can spend my time more profitably in studying."

"Do you think Mr. Gale will return?"

"He has promised to do so. I am to see him off tomorrow."

"Are you going to trust that boy alone in New York?" asked his Aunt Jane with asperity.

"Why, what could happen to me?" asked Andy indignantly.

"You might get run over."

"I am not a little boy, Aunt Jane. I can take care of myself."

"You may meet with an accident for all your smartness."

"I think Andy is old enough to take care of himself," said his father mildly.

"Oh, well! Have it your own way. You can't say but I've warned you," and she sniffed severely.

"I wonder what makes Aunt Jane so disagreeable," thought Andy.

"Perhaps you'd like to go and take care of him," suggested Mr. Grant with a smile. "You are old enough to take care of yourself."

"You needn't twit me with my age, Sterling," said Jane, with an injured sniff.

"I don't. Old age is honorable."

This made matters worse.

"You talk as if I was seventy-five. I don't consider myself an old person."

In spite of the melancholy presentiment of Aunt Jane, Andy set out for New York with Mr. Gale. An hour and a half brought them to the metropolis.

"I should like to show you something of the city, Andy," said his companion, "but I shall have to spend the time shopping."

"I shall see something of the city if I go with you."

"That is true."

At one o'clock they went to the Sinclair House, on Broadway, to dine. They selected a table where there was but one other guest, who seemed known to Walter Gale.

"Good morning, Mr. Flint," said the young man.

"Ah, it's you, Walter, is it?" returned the other, a stout man whose hair was beginning to grow gray.

"Yes."

"I haven't seen you for a long time. Where have you been?"

"Rusticating in a Connecticut town."

"Is the young man with you a brother? But, no. I remember that you have no brother."

"He isn't related to me, but I think as much of him as if he were. His name is Andrew Grant."

"A good name. Is he attending school?"

"He has recently left school."

"If he were seeking a position I could find a place for him."

"In your own employ?"

"Yes. I have a boy, but I don't find him reliable or faithful. He will leave me on Saturday night."

"Andy," said his friend, "how would you like to enter Mr. Flint's employ?"

"Very much," answered Andy eagerly.

61

At the same time he wondered what was the nature of Mr. Flint's business.

"Then after dinner we will walk together to Mr. Flint's store in Union Square."

"There is my card," said Mr. Flint.

Andy received it and read the name:

F. FLINT,
UNION SQUARE.
JEWELRY.

The two men conversed together, and when dinner was over they walked up Broadway to Fourteenth Street. Turning the left-hand corner, they soon reached a jewelry store of modest appearance but evidently containing a valuable stock.

A youth with light-brown hair, who seemed to have been born tired, was leaning against the counter. This, doubtless, was the boy who was not satisfactory.

"John," said Mr. Flint, "have you carried the parcel to Forty-eighth Street?"

"No, sir," answered the boy.

"Why not?"

"I thought it would do just as well after lunch."

"There you are mistaken. Put on your hat at once and go," said his employer sharply.

"You see," went on Mr. Flint after the boy had started, "the trouble I have with John. He needs to be looked after continually."

"You won't have that trouble with Andy."

"No, I think not."

Walter Gale accompanied Mr. Flint to the back part of the store where they held a conversation in a low tone. Presently Walter Gale came back and signified to Andy that they must be going.

"Mr. Flint will expect you to present yourself for duty on Tuesday morning," he said. "You will reach the store at eight o'clock."

"All right, sir."

On returning to the street, Walter Gale said, "I propose to take the next train for Philadelphia. You may accompany me to the Cortlandt Street station. Can you find your way from there to the Grand Central Depot?"

"Yes, sir."

"You will get there in time to take the afternoon train back to Arden. You haven't asked me what salary you are to receive."

"I should like to know, sir."

"Five dollars a week, which is better than is generally paid to a new boy."

"Will it pay my expenses, Mr. Gale?" asked Andy doubtfully.

"No, but you remember that I promised you five dollars a week. Instead of paying it to you I will give you a note to Mrs. Norris, who keeps a comfortable boarding house on Clinton Place. She knows me well and will assign you a room, looking to me for payment. That will leave you five dollars a week for your personal expenses, clothing, etc."

"I shall be rich, Mr. Gale, thanks to your kindness."

"Mind, Andy, I am to have you back whenever I want you. Probably I may spend some weeks with my uncle, and during this time you may as well work for Mr. Flint."

"Do you think I shall suit him?" asked Andy with some anxiety.

"I feel sure of it. You will find him strict in business but kind and reasonable. I shall expect to hear from you soon after you enter upon your duties. I shall find life pretty dull at my uncle's house, and your letters will bring something of the excitement of the outside world to me."

"I will write you every week, Mr. Gale."

"If it won't be asking too much of you, I shall be glad to have you do so."

Andy crossed the ferry with Mr. Gale, and then returning at once, he took the four o'clock train for Arden.

His news created considerable stir at home. All were pleased except Aunt Jane.

"Brother," she said, "are you going to trust Andy alone in New York?"

"Yes, Jane. He must begin to rely upon himself some time, and he may as well begin now."

"It's temptin' Providence, in my opinion."

"It might be so with some boys, but I have faith in Andy's prudence and good sense."

"He ain't any different from other boys, as you will find."

But in spite of these ominous words, Andy made arrangements to leave Arden on Monday morning. He looked forward eagerly to his new life in New York.

—

CHAPTER XIII

ANDY LEAVES HOME

Conrad was not slow in learning of Mr. Gale's departure from the hotel. The intelligence pleased him for, as he supposed, it threw Andy out of employment. He sought an early opportunity of speaking to him on the subject.

At five o'clock in the afternoon the mail came in at the post office. Among those who congregated there at the time were Conrad and Andy.

"So you've lost your place?" began Conrad abruptly.

"What do you mean?" asked Andy.

"Mr. Gale has left town, hasn't he?"

"Yes."

"Where has he gone?"

"To Pennsylvania, to stay with an uncle who is very sick."

"Do you think he will come back to Arden?"

"I don't know, but I think it is doubtful."

"I suppose, then, you will go back to work on the farm?"

Andy smiled. "Things might be worse," he said.

"Yes. I think it is the best thing you can do."

"Why do you think so?"

"Oh, well, you are a poor boy, and there is nothing else for you to do."

"Did you ever think of becoming a farmer?"

"I should say not," replied Conrad haughtily. "I shall probably be a lawyer or a merchant."

"I might become a merchant myself -- some day."

Conrad laughed. "When you do," he said, "let me know."

"I will."

"By the way, you won't want that boat of yours now."

"Why not?"

"You won't get time to use it. I'll give you twenty dollars for it."

"It is not for sale," answered Andy firmly.

"It will be after a while," said Conrad in a self-satisfied tone. "I will see the time when you will be glad enough to get the money I offer."

During the few days that Andy remained at home he did some work on the farm. Mr. Grant's boy helper was sick with a cold, and Andy stepped into his place.

The next time of Conrad's meeting him he was at work digging potatoes. Conrad smiled and nodded. He felt quite friendly as he witnessed what he considered Andy's humiliation.

"My father may give you a little job," he said as he leaned over the fence.

"What is it?"

"He needs some work done round the house. He will pay you fifty cents a day. When can you come?"

"Just at present I am too busy. If I can spare the time I will let you know."

"I like to see upstarts brought down to their level," thought Conrad. "Andy Grant won't be putting on anymore airs, I reckon."

On Monday morning Andy stood on the platform of the railroad station with a good-sized gripsack in his hand. He was about starting for New York to enter upon his duties at the jewelry store.

Swinging a light cane, Conrad Carter appeared on the platform with his father, who was going to the city on business. With a good deal of surprise he recognized Andy.

"Where are you going?" he asked, abruptly, with a glance at the gripsack.

"To New York," answered Andy.

"What business have you there?"

"I have a position in a store on Union Square. I shall be pleased to have you call when you are in the city."

Conrad was greatly surprised.

"What kind of a store is it?" he asked.

"A jewelry store. I haven't a card with me but will send you one."

Conrad didn't appear to be glad at Andy's good fortune. He had made up his mind that his humble rival, as he chose to consider him, would be obliged to work on the farm, and now he had found a way to avoid it.

"I think your father will have to find someone else to assist him," Andy continued. "You see, I shall be otherwise occupied."

"What pay will you receive?"

"If you will excuse me, I would rather not tell."

"Oh, just as you like. Where will you live? Will you sleep in the store?"

"No. I am to board on Clinton Place, with a Mrs. Norris."

"Did you know about this when we were talking the other day?"

"Yes."

"Why didn't you tell me?"

"I would have done so if I had known how much interest you took in my plans."

The rumble of the approaching train was heard, and Andy was obliged to enter a car. It chanced that it was unusually full, and Andy found but one vacant seat -- the one beside Squire Carter.

The squire now noticed Andy for the first time.

"Where are you going, Andrew?" he asked.

"To New York, sir."

"On any special errand?"

"I am going to work there."

"Indeed! What kind of a place?"

"I shall have a place with Mr. Flint, of Union Square, a jeweler."

"I suppose Mr. Gale obtained you the place?"

"Yes, sir."

"I am not sure that you are acting wisely. I doubt if you can make expenses. What are you to be paid?"

"Five dollars a week."

"That is very fair pay for a boy of your age, but it won't go very far in New York."

"I suppose New York is an expensive place to live in," said Andy noncommittally.

"Yes. You will have to pay all your wages for board. Your other expenses will have to come out of your father's pocket."

"I may be advanced."

"It will be a good while, first. You seem to be acting very injudiciously."

An 1880 aerial view illustration of the tip of Manhattan and the surrounding New York City area.

This remark did not trouble Andy. As his board was to be paid by Mr. Gale, his salary would be practically ten dollars a week, but this he did not care to tell.

"Country boys are always in a stew to get work in the city," observed the squire. "If they would only take the advice of their elders, they would see that it is better to stay in the country."

"They think probably that there is more chance of advancement in the city. Horace Greeley never would have risen to distinction if he had remained in his native village."

"Ahem! There are exceptions. What is the number of the store where you will be employed?"

Andy told him.

"I may call in upon you some time. I am often in the city on business."

"I shall be glad if you will," said Andy sincerely. "It will seem pleasant to me to see an Arden face."

Andy got out of the cars at the Grand Central Depot. He was not quite sure of his way to Clinton Place, but he was not in the least disturbed. He was naturally self-reliant.

He asked the question of a gentleman and was advised to take a Fourth Avenue car through the tunnel as far as Eighth Street, but he thought he should prefer to walk as it would enable him to enjoy the sights and scenes of the metropolis. All these were fresh and interesting to him.

He had gone but a dozen steps from the depot when a plausible stranger of thirty-five years, apparently, stopped him.

"Young man, may I have a word with you?" he asked.

"If you wish."

"I speak to you because I judge from your appearance that you have a good, kind heart."

"I hope you are right, sir."

"I am very awkwardly placed. My sister is very sick in Yonkers and has sent for me. On my way to the depot in a horse car I had my pocket picked, and I have not enough money to get to the bedside of my poor sister. If you would kindly lend me a quarter -- "

Andy was kind-hearted, and he was not versed in city wiles. He put his hand in his pocket and drew out a twenty-five-cent silver coin.

"I am glad to help you," he said as he passed the coin to the applicant.

"You have a noble heart. I thank you," said the stranger feelingly.

Andy felt pleased to think that he had done the man a favor, but his satisfaction was short-lived.

A stout, pleasant-looking man who had caught sight of the conference addressed him.

"Did you give that man any money?" he asked.

"Yes sir."

"What did he need it for?"

"His pocket had been picked, and he wanted to go to Yonkers to visit his sick sister."

His new friend laughed.

"That's a new story," he said. "The man is an arrant fraud. Your money will be spent for drink. He has no sick sister."

This was quite a shock to Andy. He saw that he had been victimized and must hereafter be on his guard against plausible strangers.

CHAPTER XIV

THE FIRST DAY IN NEW YORK

By dint of a little inquiry Andy found his way to Mrs. Norris' boarding house in Clinton Place. It was a plain three-story and basement house of brick and looked thoroughly respectable.

Andy took a general view of it and thought he should take it. To his country eyes it looked quite aristocratic. It was higher than any house in Arden, even Squire Carter's.

He ascended the steps and rang the bell.

It was answered by a Swedish girl named Eva, a blond girl of the true Scandinavian type.

"Is Mrs. Norris at home?" he asked.

"She is upstairs," was the reply.

"I should like to see her."

"Who shall I tell her calls?"

"She won't know my name. Tell her it is someone with a letter from Mr. Walter Gale."

"Won't you step in?"

She ushered Andy into a small reception room opening from the hall. It was a very small room with a sofa, one chair and a writing desk. Just over the sofa hung an engraving of Washington crossing the Delaware.

Andy sat down on the sofa and placed his gripsack in front of him. There was nothing to occupy his mind, so he sat patiently, wondering what sort of a looking woman the landlady might be.

Soon there was a rustle of garments, and a stout, pleasant-looking lady, of perhaps fifty and wearing a small cap set off with red ribbons, entered the room.

"Mrs. Norris?" said Andy inquiringly, rising out of respect.

"Yes, I am Mrs. Norris. Eva told me you had a letter from Mr. -- I didn't catch the name."

"Mr. Walter Gale."

"Oh, yes, Mr. Gale. I know him very well."

"Did he ever board here?"

"No. He boarded at one of the hotels. Mr. Gale is a rich man."

She took the letter and read it.

"Mr. Gale asks if I can take you to board and offers to pay your board. He must be a great friend of yours?"

"He is. I hope the arrangement will be satisfactory."

"Quite so. I couldn't wish any better paymaster than Mr. Gale. Are you going to work in the city?"

"Yes. I have a place in Mr. Flint's jewelry store on Union Square."

"Really? That is quite a high-toned place. I got my best spoons there."

"Have you got a room for me?" asked Andy a little anxiously.

"Yes, I've got a small hall bedroom. I suppose you didn't expect a square room?"

"It would be too expensive."

"It wouldn't be if you had a roommate. There's a gentleman on the third floor front, a Mr. Warren. He is sickly and writes for some of the papers. He told me he would like a roommate, but perhaps you would prefer a small room alone?"

"I should."

"Then I've a small room on the same floor. It was occupied till last week by a music teacher, but he was three weeks behind in his rent and I had to let him go. It's a trying business, keeping a boarding house, Mr. -- "

"Grant," suggested Andy.

"Yes. That's a good name. I suppose you're in nowise related to the general?"

"No. I wish I was."

"If you will follow me upstairs I'll show you the room. You can bring your valise."

Andy took it in his hand and followed the landlady up two flights of stairs. She panted a little, being a stout lady, but Andy would have run upstairs if he had been alone.

On the upper floor there were three rooms, the doors of all being open.

"That is Mr. Warren's room," said Mrs. Norris pointing to the front apartment.

It was a room of about fourteen feet square and was neatly furnished. It contained a double bed and the usual chamber furniture.

"It will accommodate two gentlemen nicely," said Mrs. Norris. "Perhaps, after you get acquainted with Mr. Warren, you may strike up a bargain to room with him."

"I don't think I should like to room with a sickly gentleman."

"Well, there is something in that. One night Mr. Warren had a fit -- I don't know what kind of one -- and rolled onto the floor. I room just underneath, and I was very much frightened."

"It would have frightened me, too, if I had roomed with him."

"Well, fits ain't very pleasant, I allow."

"Who rooms in the third room, next to mine?"

"A young man of eighteen, named Perkins. I don't rightly know what sort of a place he is in. I think it's a neckwear store on Spring Street."

Andy was rather glad to learn that there was one boarder somewhere near his own age.

He did not think he should enjoy the acquaintance of Mr. Warren. He was prejudiced against him by the knowledge that he was sickly and had fits.

"There are other boarders on my second floor. You will make their acquaintance at the table."

"What are your hours for meals, Mrs. Norris?"

"We have lunch from twelve to one. Breakfast is from seven to nine, and we have dinner from six to seven, though in the case of a boarder who is kept later by business we stretch a point, and try to accommodate him. I hope that will suit you."

"Oh, I am sure it will."

"Shall you be at lunch today?"

"No, I don't think so. I am going to explore the city a little."

"Very few of my boarders are present at lunch. Still there is a bite for them, if they do come."

"I would like to wash, if you will send up some water and a towel."

"Eva will bring them right up. Have you soap of your own?"

"Yes."

"Gentlemen often prefer providing their own. If you will give me your name in full, I will enter it on my books."

"My name is Andrew Grant."

"Very well."

"What is your rate of board? Mr. Gale will pay it, but I should like to know what it is."

"Five dollars a week for your room. Mr. Warren pays seven, but he has a large room to himself. If you should decide to room with him, I shall charge you five dollars apiece."

"Thank you. I don't think we shall come to any agreement."

She went downstairs, and Andy surveyed his room with interest.

It was certainly small -- quite the narrowest room he had ever seen. There was one window from which he had a view of the backyard, rather a forlorn-looking space. There was a cat perched on the high, board fence separating the yard from that of the adjoining house.

Andy liked cats, and called out "Kitty." The cat looked up and mewed her recognition and acknowledgment of the friendly overture. Then Eva came up with a pitcher of water and a towel.

"Will one do you?" she asked. "The rest are in the wash, and I'll bring you another this evening."

"One will be sufficient for the present."

"So you're comin' here to live?" she said sociably.

"Yes, Eva."

"I hope you don't have fits, like Mr. Warren."

"I don't think I ever had one yet," answered Andy with a smile.

"I'm glad of that. I'm afraid of gentlemen that have fits."

Eva went downstairs, and Andy proceeded to make his ablutions. It was a dusty day, and the water was refreshing.

After he had washed his face and hands he opened his gripsack and took out his brush and comb, which he placed on a tiny bureau in one corner of the room. It contained two drawers, and in one of them he put away the contents of the valise.

By this time it was half-past ten, and he put on his hat and went downstairs. He went out into the street, and after a moment of indecision walked to Broadway. He thought he could not do better than to walk down this wonderful thoroughfare, of which he had heard so much.

It did occur to him that he might report at the jewelry store, but he would see enough of that hereafter and he preferred to take a little walk about the city.

Andy used his eyes to good advantage. He looked in at the shop windows and watched the human tide that swept by him.

Finally he found himself accosted by one of the passersby.

"My young friend, could you oblige me with a quarter to take me to Newark? My pocket has been picked, and -- "

All this seemed familiar. Andy looked up and recognized at once the stranger whom he had met in front of the Grand Central Depot.

"When did you get back from Yonkers?" he asked abruptly.

72

"I never was in Yonkers."

"I gave you a quarter only an hour or two ago to get to your sick sister in Yonkers."

Muttering that there was some mistake, the man hurried away looking confused.

"I wonder if I shall ever meet him again?" thought Andy.

CHAPTER XV

ANDY'S OPPOSITE NEIGHBOR

Andy walked about the city using his eyes industriously. At one o'clock he went into a restaurant on Park Row where he got a fair lunch for twenty-five cents.

This was more than he intended to pay usually, but on this first day in the city he did not care to go back to the boarding house.

After lunch he made his way to the entrance of the Brooklyn Bridge and got into one of the cars. He enjoyed the prospect visible from the windows and felt that this alone would pay him for visiting New York.

The streets of Manhattan in the late 1800s

Just before they reached the other end there was a cry of alarm from a stout German woman who sat on the other side of the car.

"I've been robbed!" she exclaimed. "My purse is gone!"
Of course this attracted general attention.

"Was there much in the purse, madam?" asked a kind-looking, elderly man.

"Yes, there was six dollars -- it was a great deal to me."

"Are you sure you had it when you entered the car?"

"Yes. I took it out of my pocket when I paid for a ticket."

"I think your pocket must have been picked."

Sitting next to the woman was a man who seemed absorbed in reading a morning newspaper; even the woman's complaint did not appear to excite his attention.

This led Andy to move his head to get a nearer view of him. He started in surprise. It was the adventurer, whom he had already met twice that morning. He had little doubt that he was the thief.

It was perhaps somewhat rash to hazard a charge without proof, but he felt indignant and could not resist the impulse.

"I think that man has your purse," he said pointing to the individual behind the newspaper.

"This is an outrage!" exclaimed the latter with assumed anger. "I am a Boston merchant."

He was respectably dressed, and the charge did not seem very plausible.

"My boy, you should be careful how you make such charges," said his next neighbor reprovingly.

But Andy was not abashed.

"I know something of that man," he said quietly. "I have met him twice this morning."

"Has he robbed you?"

"No, but he asked me to give him a quarter to take him to his sick sister in Yonkers. This was at the Grand Central Depot. An hour or two later I met him on Broadway, and he wanted money to take him to Newark."

"The boy is entirely mistaken," said the adventurer.

At the same instant, under cover of the newspaper, he adroitly let the stolen purse drop to the floor at his feet.

By this time the cars had reached the Brooklyn end of the bridge.

"Why, there is your purse," exclaimed the adventurer with a sudden glance downward. "You must have dropped it."

"Oh, thank you, sir!" said the poor woman overjoyed.

"I hope you won't suspect a gentleman again," said the thief in lofty indignation.

"No, I won't, sir. I was sure you didn't take it."

Andy, who had seen the trick, smiled, but he was satisfied with the recovery of the purse.

The passengers looked puzzled. They had not made up their minds as to the guilt or innocence of the man charge with the theft.

"You see, young man," said Andy's neighbor in a tone of reproof, "you were mistaken."

Andy smiled again.

"I saw him drop the purse on the floor," he answered quietly.

"Bless my soul! Are you sure?"

"Yes, sir."

The passengers left the car, Andy and the thief among them.

Andy lost track of his acquaintance till, as they reached Fulton Street, he heard some one hissing in his ear, "Boy, you are too fresh! I'll get even with you yet!"

Then the thief, passing him rapidly, got into a Myrtle Avenue car, and this was the last he saw of him for that day.

Andy walked about the streets of Brooklyn for a while and returned by Fulton Ferry. Then he went back to his boarding place, arriving there between three and four o'clock.

As he went up to his room he noticed that the door of the large room opposite was open. A young man, of about thirty, was sitting in a rocking chair, reading.

He was of medium height and sallow complexion. He wore his hair long and had a high, narrow forehead.

"I suppose that is the man who has fits," thought Andy.

The young man had noticed Andy's entrance into his own room and, rising from the rocking chair, crossed the hall and knocked lightly at the door.

"Come in," said Andy.

"I suppose this is Mr. Grant," began the young man bowing. "I am Mr. Warren and live in the room opposite."

"Won't you come in and sit down?" asked Andy with a glance at the only chair the room contained.

"Don't let me take your only chair. I'll sit on the bed, if you don't mind."

"Make yourself at home, Mr. Warren," said Andy with easy cordiality.

"So you know my name?"

"Mrs. Norris spoke to me of you."

"Did she? What did she say?" asked the young man showing some curiosity.

76

"I think she said you were literary -- that you wrote for some of the magazines."

"Yes. I am very fond of writing. Do you write?"

"Not for publication."

"Ah, yes, I see. You would be rather young for an author."

"Are you connected with any particular magazine?"

"No. I a freelance. I contribute to several. I have just sent an article to the Century."

Andy was rather surprised, for he knew that the Century held high rank among contemporary magazines. It did not occur to him that any one might send an article to that magazine, but that to have it accepted and published would be a different matter.

"I suppose you enjoy writing?"

"Yes. There is nothing I like so well."

"Perhaps you will show me some of your articles."

"I can show you a poem which appeared last week in the village paper at home."

"Thank you, I should like to see it."

Mr. Warren went up to his room and speedily returned with a small weekly paper.

On the front page at the head of the first column was a short poem by G. Byron Warren. This was the first stanza, which Mr. Warren volunteered to read aloud:

"'I'd like to be a robin,
And flit from bough to bough;
I'd pour sweet music on the air
If God would teach me how.'"

"I don't quite like that last line," he said looking up from the paper. "Can you suggest any improvement?"

"You might say, 'And charm the pensive cow,'" suggested Andy mischievously.

"True, that might be a striking figure. I will consider it when I revise the poem for publication in book form."

The rest of the poem was of similar quality.

"I don't think they would accept that for the Century," thought Andy.

"Do you devote yourself to literary work, or are you in business?" he asked.

"I may go into business, but at present I only write. I send a letter once a month to the Greenville Banner."

"I suppose they pay?"

"Oh -- eh, yes," answered the poet, in a hesitating voice, "but the terms are strictly confidential. If you ever pick up any incidents in your daily walks, Mr. Grant, I shall be glad if you will communicate them to me so that I may weave them into my correspondence."

"With pleasure."

Then it occurred to Andy to tell his neighbor about the street adventurer whom he had met three times that morning.

"Capital!" exclaimed Warren. "I will get that into my next letter. I see, Mr. Grant, you have an observing eye. You would make a good reporter for one of the city dailies."

"Do you think so?" asked Andy feeling complimented.

"I am sure of it."

"How long have you lived in the city, Mr. Warren?"

"About three months. Some time I will tell you why I came here," he continued, with an air of mystery.

"I shall be glad to hear."

"I will tell you now, for I see you have a sympathetic soul. I loved, and my love was returned, but a heartless parent interposed and separated two loving hearts."

He took out his handkerchief and wiped his eyes. Andy hardly knew whether to laugh or to express sympathy.

"I suppose that often happens?" he said rather lamely. "Perhaps he may yet repent."

"I live in that hope. When I have become famous, I will go back and offer myself again to Sophia. I suppose you have had no heart experiences as yet, Mr. Grant?"

"Not as yet, but I can sympathize with you."

"I am so glad you have come. I shall make you my confidential friend."

Then the conversation drifted into other channels.

CHAPTER XVI

ANDY AT WORK

Punctually as the clock struck eight the next morning, Andy entered the store of Mr. Flint on Union Square. He looked for his employer, but the jeweler seldom arrived before nine, his residence being in Harlem.

Behind the counter, arranging the goods in one of the cases, was a man with reddish hair who might at a guess be thirty-five years of age. It was Mr. Flint's head clerk, Simon Rich, who had been absent when Andy made his first call.

"What can I do for you, boy?" he asked superciliously.

"Is Mr. Flint in?"

"No. You can tell me your business."

"I have come here to work."

"Ohhhh!"

This exclamation was long-drawn out. Mr. Rich then proceeded to examine Andy from head to foot in a manner which was extremely offensive.

Andy understood that for some reason this man would be his enemy. He would have understood his hostility better had he known that the boy just discharged was the head clerk's nephew.

"I suppose you are well acquainted with the business?" remarked Rich with a sneer.

"I know nothing about it."

"Humph! You stand a chance of being very useful."

"I hope to become familiar with it soon," said Andy coloring.

"Suppose you sweep, to begin with."

He pointed out the broom, and Andy went to work.

"I wish he were a more agreeable man," thought Andy. "I am afraid he will make my position unpleasant."

Here a customer came in, and Mr. Rich was occupied for the next ten minutes.

The customer, a lady, bought a gold chain.

"Shall I send it?" asked the clerk.

"Yes, but not till twelve o'clock."

"To what address?"

She gave a number on Fifty-Sixth Street.

"Very well."

"There will be an errand for you," said Rich as he put back the chains not selected.

Andy nodded. He felt that he would rather be absent on an errand than in the company of Simon Rich.

"Where did Mr. Flint pick you up?" inquired Rich.

This was rude, but Andy felt that it would not be politic to get into a quarrel with the head clerk so soon.

"We met at lunch," he said.

"Where?"

"At the Sinclair House."

"Had you never seen him before?"

"No."

"Queer that he should engage you at such short notice!"

"He was acquainted with the gentleman I was with."

"What name?"

"Walter Gale."

"Yes, I have seen him. Are you related to Mr. Gale?"

"No."

"Are you aware that the boy you have displaced -- John Crandall -- is my nephew?"

"No, sir. I didn't know it. I am sorry he has lost his place."

"He is a good boy, but Mr. Flint became prejudiced against him. Did he say anything about him when he engaged you?"

"I believe he said that he was not satisfactory, but as I did not know him I did not notice."

Another customer came in, and at nine o'clock Mr. Flint entered.

"I see you are on hand," he said pleasantly to Andy.

"Yes, sir."

"When did you come to the city?"

"Yesterday, sir."

"Have you a boarding place?"

"Yes, sir, in Clinton Place. I was recommended to it by Mr. Gale."

"That is well. Mr. Rich, this is the new boy."

"So he told me," said Rich coldly.

"Have you had any customers?"

"Yes, sir. There is one article to be sent -- a gold chain -- to Mrs. Mason of Fifty-Sixth Street."

"Any time mentioned?"

"Twelve o'clock."

"You can send Andrew at that time."

"Very well, sir."

Andy was very glad of his employer's presence. It checked any manifestation of rudeness on the part of the clerk.

At quarter to twelve a box containing the chain was handed to Andy, addressed to Mrs. Mason.

"Did you notice the lady who purchased the chain?" asked Mr. Flint.

"Yes, sir."

"I wish this box placed in her hands. Ask her to give you a receipt for it."

"Yes, sir."

"Here is money for car fare. You may go to lunch after delivering the box."

"Yes, sir."

Andy took a Broadway car, and just after twelve reached the house. The door was opened by a man-servant.

"I have a parcel for Mrs. Mason," said Andy.

"All right. I'll take it."

"I am only to deliver it into her hands."

"She isn't at home."

"Then I will wait for her. She said she would be here at twelve."

The man was about to speak rudely, when a lady mounted the steps.

"Are you from Mr. Flint?" she asked.

"Yes, madam."

"I am Mrs. Mason."

"I remember you," said Andy bowing. "Will you be kind enough to give me a receipt?"

"Certainly. Step into the hall, and I won't keep you waiting long."

Andy sat down.

"Why didn't you give me the parcel, boy?" asked the servant.

"Because you are not Mrs. Mason. I had strict orders to deliver it to her."

"Humph! That is being mighty particular."

"I have nothing to do with Mr. Flint's rules."

Mrs. Mason returned almost immediately.

"Here is the receipt, and thank you," she said pleasantly.

81

Andy bowed and opened the door to go out.

"I am afraid I have interfered with your lunch," she said.

"I am going to it now, thank you."

"My lunch is just ready. Perhaps you will accept an invitation to lunch with me?"

"I shall be very glad to do so."

Andy had been brought up as a gentleman and was not at all embarrassed, as some boys would have been, by this attention from a lady.

"Follow me, then," she said as she led the way downstairs to the front basement.

A small table was set there, and Mrs. Mason pointed to a seat.

"You are my only guest," she said. "My boy is out of town just at present. Shall I help you to some cold chicken?"

"Thank you."

Besides the chicken there was bread and butter, some kind of preserve, and hot tea. It was all very plain, but Andy enjoyed it.

"I ought to know the name of my guest," said Mrs. Mason.

"My name is Andrew Grant."

"Have you been long at Mr. Flint's?"

"This is my first day."

"I hope you will find the situation a pleasant one. You are not a city boy?"

"No, I came from Arden."

They were waited upon at table by Gustave, the man who had treated Andy rudely.

He did not look at all pleasant at having to wait upon the boy from "Flint's," and he evidently considered his mistress very eccentric.

Mrs. Mason gossiped pleasantly and evidently enjoyed her young company.

"That is better than eating alone," she said as she rose from the table. "I feel quite well acquainted with you, Andrew. You must come up sometime when my boy is at home. He is a year or two younger than you, but I think you will get on together."

"I shall be very glad to come," replied Andy gratefully. "Thank you for all your kindness."

He went back to the store at once.

"You are back early," said Mr. Flint.

"Yes, sir. Mrs. Mason invited me to lunch and that saved time."

Simon Rich looked surprised. His nephew had never received so much attention from a customer.

CHAPTER XVII

ANDY'S FELLOW BOARDERS

As time went on, Andy became aware that Simon Rich was indeed no friend of his. He was watched with a cold vigilance that was nothing less than a lookout for imperfections. Andy saw that it would be necessary for him to be unusually careful and attentive to his duties.

Mr. Flint, on the other hand, was always kind and cordial, notwithstanding the slighting words from Mr. Rich.

One day when Andy returned from lunch he found a boy talking with Simon Rich. He recognized him as his predecessor.

The boy, John Crandall, looked at him with an ill-natured glance. As Simon Rich did not see fit to introduce him he did not speak. When Rich went out to lunch John Crandall accompanied him.

"Don't you think there is any chance of my getting back, Uncle Simon?" asked John.

"Not at present. That boy you saw seems to have the inside track with Mr. Flint."

"What sort of a boy is he?"

"He's too fresh. I don't like him."

"What made Mr. Flint take him on?"

"Heaven knows; I don't."

"Do you think he is likely to stay?"

"Not if I can help it."

"Can't you prejudice Mr. Flint against him?"

"I will if I can. I am looking for a chance to get him into trouble, but it isn't easy, as he is a goody-goody sort of a boy. He tries to get in with people. You know Mrs. Mason, of Fifty-Sixth Street?"

"Yes. I have carried purchases there."

"The very first day he was here he went there with a chain, and she invited him to lunch."

"You don't mean it?" exclaimed John in surprise. "She never took any notice of me."

They went to the Dairy Restaurant on Union Square for lunch.

"Uncle Simon," said John when they were going out, "can't you give me fifty cents? You know I haven't a cent of money, now that my salary has stopped."

"What do you want fifty cents for?" demanded his uncle frowning.

"I want to go to the Grand Opera House tonight. I haven't been to the theater for two weeks."

"And you can't expect to while you are not earning anything."

"But that isn't my fault," pleaded John.

"Yes, it is. You neglected your duties at Flint's, and he saw it. That is why you lost your place."

"It is pretty hard going about without a cent of money in your pocket."

"Then you should have kept your place. Have you been around to look for another position?"

"No. I thought you would get me back into Flint's."

"I don't think there is much chance, but I will try to get the other boy out."

"I hope you'll do that. I hate the sight of him. I feel as if he had turned me out of my place."

"How do you like the new boy, Mr. Rich?" asked the jeweler at the end of the first week.

"I don't care much for him," said Simon Rich coldly.

"What is the matter with him? Does he neglect his work?"

"No," Rich admitted unwillingly.

"What have you against him, then?"

"He has a sneaking way about him."

"On the contrary, he seems to me to be unusually frank and open."

"He is trying to get into your good graces."

"Well, that is proper, isn't it?

"Yes, but -- "

"Well?"

"I think he will bear watching."

"Surely you don't suspect him of dishonesty."

"Still waters run deep," said the clerk sententiously.

Mr. Flint smiled to himself as he turned away. He understood that the secret of his head clerk's prejudice was the fact that Andy had taken the place of his nephew.

Meanwhile Andy had got well acquainted at his boarding house. Besides Mr. Warren he found his next neighbor, Sam Perkins, quite sociable.

Sam was a youth of eighteen and was employed in a furnishing-goods store on lower Broadway. He was fortunate in the location of his store, as he finished work at half-past five and was able to be at supper at the regular hour. He seemed rather fond of dress and indulged in a variety of showy neckties, being able to get them at wholesale rates.

He introduced himself to Andy the first evening.

"What pay do you get?" he asked.

"Five dollars a week."

"I get seven, but it's too small. A man can't live on it. Why, my car fare costs me sixty cents a week."

"It must be rather a tight squeeze."

"The folks at home allow me two dollars a week besides. You see, the governor's got money. But I tell you money melts away in New York."

"No doubt. There are a good many ways of spending money here."

"Suppose we go to the theater tonight."

"I would rather wait a while. This is my first night in the city."

"Have you got acquainted with old Warren?"

"You mean the occupant of the large room opposite?"

"Yes."

"I have talked with him a little."

"How do you like him?"

"I don't know him well enough to judge," said Andy cautiously.

"He's a crank -- and soft at that. Pretends that he is literary and writes for the magazines."

"He does, doesn't he?"

"Yes, he writes for them, but I don't think his articles get printed. He just sits round and writes and isn't any company at all. I have tried to get him to go to the theater, but he won't. Once I was hard up -- hadn't but a nickel -- and asked him to lend me a quarter. He wouldn't."

"Very likely he hasn't got much money."

"That's right. Did you ever see such shabby neckties as he wears?"

"He hasn't your advantages about getting new neckties," said Andy with a smile, for he had already learned where Sam was at work.

"How do you like the tie I have on? It's a stunner, isn't it?" asked Sam complacently.

"It's very showy."

"I get a new necktie every week. You see, I get them at half price. Girls always notice your necktie."

"Then I don't think they'll pay me much attention."

"Your tie is too sober, that's a fact. Better let me bring you one. I can get it half off. They won't know but it's for me."

"Thank you. I may by and by accept your offer. Now, I don't want to spend any extra money."

At the table Andy was introduced to a Mr. and Mrs. Osborn, who did not appear to be long married. She was tall, angular and thirty-five. He was at least five years younger. He had married her for her money, but she let him have little advantage of it, dealing it out in small sums.

He occupied a small clerkship at eight dollars a week, out of which he had to pay his own board, while his wife, who had an income from property of a thousand dollars a year, defrayed her own expenses and occasionally allowed him a dollar or two.

He was much better looking than his wife, and it was this, perhaps, that made her jealous if he looked at another woman. The particular object of her jealousy was a Miss Manson, who held a business position at an uptown milliner's. She was pleasant and piquant.

There was also a Mr. Kimball, who was a salesman at Hearn's. He liked to discuss financial problems and felt that he should have been a banker, but he found no one to talk with, as Mr. Osborn's ideas on finance were elementary.

Indeed, Mrs. Osborn was the only one at the table who was competent to converse with him on his favorite subject.

"Miss Manson, may I pass you the sugar?" asked Mr. Osborn on the first occasion of Andy's appearing at dinner.

"Miss Manson can reach the sugar bowl herself," interposed Mrs. Osborn, with a reproving frown.

"I like to be neighborly, my dear," said her husband deprecatingly.

"I see you do."

Miss Manson smiled, and so did others at the table, who detected Mrs. Osborn's jealousy.

"Have you read the President's financial message, Mr. Osborn?" asked Mr. Kimball.

"No. I don't take any interest in such things."

"I have read it, Mr. Kimball," said Mrs. Osborn, "and I approve his recommendations."

"So do I, with one exception," returned Mr. Kimball, and they began a conversation in which none of the other boarders took an interest.

When supper was over, Andy and Sam went for a walk. Mr. Warren excused himself on the ground that he was writing a poem for one of the magazines.

"So you are with a jeweler," said Sam. "I may come up and buy a ring some day. Do you allow a discount to friends?"

"I don't know yet. I will favor you if I can."

CHAPTER XVIII

A PLOT AGAINST ANDY

Some six weeks later, about the middle of the forenoon, a Western Union Telegraph boy entered the store and handed Mr. Flint a telegram.

Tearing it open, the jeweler read the contents and seemed quite agitated.

"Mr. Rich," he said turning to the head clerk, "I have bad news. My only brother is dangerously sick. This dispatch says that if I wish to see him alive I must start at once."

"Where does he live?"

"In Denver, Colorado."

"That is a long way off."

"Yes. I don't see how I can leave the business, but I cannot bear to think of my brother dying without my seeing him again."

"I think, sir, that I can keep things straight. I have been with you for six years."

"True, and you know the business thoroughly. Besides, you can write or telegraph me, if need be, every day."

"I will do so, sir. You can depend on me."

"Besides, you will have Andrew to help you. He is a good and faithful boy."

To this Simon Rich made no reply, but there was a look on his face that boded no good for Andy.

"I think I will go home at once and get ready. It is necessary that I should start immediately. I shall have no time to give you directions, but I will write you as soon as I reach Denver."

"Very well, sir," said Simon Rich smoothly. "Put your mind at ease. All will go well during your absence."

Half an hour later, when Andy returned from an errand, Mr. Flint was gone.

"I have a message for Mr. Flint," said Andy as he entered the store.

"You can give it to me."

"I was told to deliver it to Mr. Flint personally."

"You will find that rather a hard job, young man," said Rich with a sneer.

"I don't understand you," returned Andy in surprise.

"Mr. Flint is on his way to Denver by this time."

"Does he go on business?"

"He has received news that his only brother lies there at the point of death."

"How long will he be gone?" asked Andy, who began to understand that this was likely to prove bad news for him.

"Probably not less than three weeks. Of course, I shall manage the store while he is away. Did you hear that?"

"Yes."

"And I want you to understand," continued Rich in a bullying tone, "that I won't stand any nonsense from you. You will have to attend strictly to business. I sha'n't be such an easy-going boss as Mr. Flint."

"I always aim to do my duty," said Andy.

"You will find it best to do so while I am in charge. Now, don't stand gaping there, but go to work."

Andy was moved to an angry reply, but thought it prudent to refrain. He realized that for three weeks, and probably longer, he was to be at the mercy of a man who evidently disliked him.

How he should be able to stand it he did not know. He determined, however, to do his duty as well as he knew how, and not to reply when the head clerk was insolent and abusive.

About an hour later Simon Rich gave him a letter, which he directed him to drop in the nearest mail box.

It was addressed to John Crandall, Andy's predecessor, and ran thus:

DEAR JOHN:

Come around as soon as you can. I have news for you.

Your uncle,

SIMON RICH.

About four o'clock John Crandall entered the store.

"Andrew," said Rich, "you may go to the branch post office at Ninth Street and get a dollar's worth of postage stamps."

Andy understood that stamps were not needed and that the errand was devised to get him out of the way. However it was his duty to obey.

When he was fairly out of the store, John asked, with some curiosity:

"What is the news you were going to tell me, Uncle Simon?"

"Mr. Flint has started for Colorado, and I am in full charge of the store," answered Rich with a triumphant smile.

"Golly! That's great news!" exclaimed John. "Now you can discharge that cub and get me in again."

"I mean to, but you will have to wait a few days."

"Why need I?"

"Because I must have a good excuse for bouncing him. Mr. Flint will inquire, you know."

"I should think it would be easy to invent one."

"Well, not altogether easy, but I have a plan. You see, the boy is one of the goody-goody kind who has no bad habits. If I could catch him playing pool, or anything of that kind, there would be no trouble, but he is one of your model boys."

"Like me," suggested John.

"I never took you for a model boy. Still, you are my nephew, and I must do the best I can for you."

"What is the plan you have thought of?"

"I haven't fully decided, but come in tomorrow, and I may think of something by that time."

"I wish I was here now. It will be good fun, now that old Flint is gone."

"Be careful not to say 'old Flint' before Andrew. He might repeat it to the boss when he returns."

"If he should I would punch his head," said John promptly.

"I don't think I would advise you to do that," said Simon Rich shrewdly.

"Why not? I could lick him with one hand."

"If you ever get into a fight with him you will need two. He is strong and muscular."

"You seem to be taking his part, Uncle Simon."

"Not at all, but I won't shut my eyes to facts. Andrew is much stronger than you are."

John did not look well pleased, but his uncle added, "In this case, however, it is not a matter of strength. We must use cunning."

"All right, uncle. You know best, of course."

"Of course I know best. All you have to do is to be guided by me. We must get rid of him in such a way that Mr. Flint will approve of my action."

"It will be a great day for me when I take his place."

"Exactly. Be patient, and it will come about. Meanwhile I want you to treat him as a friend."

"Why?"

"So that he won't suspect that there is any conspiracy against him."

"I see. You are a smart one, Uncle Simon."

"I flatter myself that I know what I am about," returned Rich complacently.

Andy was considerably surprised at the kindness with which he was treated, during the next few days, by the head salesman. He had expected something very different. He began to think he had misjudged Mr. Rich.

He was still more surprised when the next day at his lunch hour he was invited to the Dairy Kitchen by John Crandall. He did not care to accept, but John insisted upon it, and he thought it would be rude to refuse.

John chatted very pleasantly during the meal, and Andy was both surprised and pleased.

"Have you got a new place?" he asked.

"No, but uncle thinks he can get me one before long."

"I hope it will be a good one."

"Oh, I think it will," said John, showing his teeth and smiling significantly.

So passed several days, and Andy began to think that Mr. Rich had become his friend. But at length the storm broke.

One day, as he entered the store, he noticed that Simon Rich was looking grave and stern.

"Andrew," he said without preface, "something very disagreeable has happened."

"What is it, Mr. Rich?"

"A gold watch has disappeared from this case."

"A valuable one?" asked Andy innocently.

"It is one that retails at fifty dollars. I would not have had this occur during Mr. Flint's absence for twice that sum."

"Have you any idea of what has become of it?"

"Not at present, but as you and my nephew are in the store so much, of course you would have opportunities of taking it."

"Uncle Simon," said John who was present, "I insist on your searching me."

"I will do so, though I am sure neither you nor Andrew is at fault."

"Search me, too, Mr. Rich," said Andy fearlessly.

Nothing was found on John, but thrusting his hand into the upper pocket of Andy's vest, Simon Rich drew out a folded paper.

"What is this?" he cried. "A pawn ticket for a gold watch? What does this mean?"

"Let me see it," said Andy dumbfounded.

It was a ticket issued by a Third Avenue pawnbroker for a gold watch, on which ten dollars appeared to have been loaned. The name of the borrower appeared as A. Grant.

"Miserable boy!" said the salesman severely. "So you have turned thief. What a hypocrite you must be!"

"I don't know what it means," faltered Andy quite overwhelmed.

CHAPTER XIX

ANDY IS DISCHARGED

"You don't know what it means!" repeated Simon Rich in a sarcastic tone. "Probably not. I understand it."

"Do you think I stole a watch and pawned it, Mr. Rich?" demanded Andy with spirit.

"There seems to be absolute proof of your dishonesty. Will you explain how, otherwise, this pawn ticket is found in your pocket?"

"I can't explain it, nor can I understand it. All I can say is, that I never saw it before."

"You must think I am a fool to be deceived by such a story."

"I can't believe that Andy pawned a watch," said John Crandall hypocritically.

"Will you be kind enough to inform me who did, then?" asked his uncle with pretended severity.

"I can't guess."

"Nor any one else, I fancy. Of course, Andrew, after this proof of your dishonesty, I cannot retain you in my, or rather in Mr. Flint's, employment."

"Mr. Rich, will you do me a favor?"

"What is it?"

"Will you go with me to the pawnbroker who issued the ticket and ask him if he ever saw me before?"

"I have no time to go on such a foolish errand. Can you give me the ten dollars you obtained for the watch?"

"I didn't obtain a dollar nor a cent for the watch. I know nothing about it."

"Probably you have laid it away somewhere or spent it."

"That is not true, and I am sure you don't believe it yourself."

"No impudence, young man! I am forced to believe it. I have treated you kindly since Mr. Flint went away, and that is sufficient to show that I wish to do you no injustice. Is this true or not?"

"I have no fault to find with your treatment, except now."

"I shall continue to act as your friend. I might have you arrested, and your conviction would be certain with the evidence I have in my possession. But I will not do it. I will redeem the watch at my own expense and be content with discharging you."

"I believe there is a plot against me," said Andy, pale but firm. "It will come out some time. When do you wish me to go?"

"At once. I will pay you to the end of the week, but I could not feel safe in retaining your services any longer. John, will you oblige me by taking Andrew's place till I have a chance to secure another boy?"

"Yes, Uncle Simon, but I don't want to feel that I have had anything to do with Andy's discharge."

"You have not. No one is responsible for it but himself."

"Then I will stay while you need me. I don't want to leave you in a hole."

Simon Rich went to the money drawer and drew out a five-dollar bill.

"Here is your pay to the end of the week," he said.

"I prefer to accept pay only to today," replied Andy.

"As you please."

Andy walked out of the store feeling crushed and overwhelmed. He was all at sea concerning the pawn ticket. He could not understand how it got into his pocket.

He formed a resolution. He would go around to the pawnbroker's and see if he could obtain any information.

He found the pawn shop without difficulty. It was a small apartment but seemed quite full of goods of all varieties.

A small man of perhaps sixty was behind the counter. Seated in a rocking chair, sewing, an old lady was to be seen in the rear of the shop.

Andy had never before been in a pawn shop and would have been interested in examining it if his errand had not been so serious.

He walked up to the counter.

"Well, young man, what is your business?" asked the old man.

"Do you remember lending some money on a new gold watch last Monday?"

"Was the watch stolen?" asked the pawnbroker, with a shade of anxiety.

"You will have no difficulty about it. It will be redeemed."

"How much did I lend on it?"

"Ten dollars."

"Yes, I remember."

"Can you remember who brought it in?"

"No, except that it was a boy about your size."

"Did he look like me?"

"I can't remember. You see, I have so many customers."

"I remember," said the old lady speaking up. "He was about your size."

"It was not I?"

"No. He was thinner than you, and he was dark complexioned."

A light began to dawn upon Andy. This description fit John Crandall.

"Do you remember what kind of an overcoat he wore?"

"It was a light overcoat."

"Thank you. Will you please remember this if you are asked?"

"Did the young gentleman own the watch?"

"He was employed by another party, but I cannot tell you any more at present. The watch will probably be redeemed by a man of about thirty-five. Don't mention to him that anyone has asked you questions about it."

"All right. I shall be glad to oblige you. You are sure it was not stolen?"

"The man who sent the boy was not dishonest. You will have no trouble."

"It was a new watch, and I thought it might be stolen. We poor pawnbrokers have a hard time. If we take stolen property we get into trouble, but how can we tell if the rings and watches they bring in are stolen?"

"Very true. I can see that you must sometimes be puzzled. Do those who pawn articles generally give their own names?"

"Very seldom. They almost always give wrong names. That sometimes leads to trouble. I remember a gentleman who mislaid his ticket, and he could not remember what name he gave. If he had we might have overlooked the loss of the pawn ticket. As it was, we did not know but he might be a fraud, though I think it was all right, and the watch he pawned was his own."

A 19th century gold watch

"Thank you for answering my questions. I am sorry to have troubled you," said Andy politely.

"Oh, it is no matter," rejoined the old man, who felt very favorably impressed by Andy's good looks and frank, open manner.

As Andy went out of the shop he experienced a feeling of relief. He saw that he would be able to prove his innocence through the testimony of the pawnbroker and his wife. He was in no hurry. It would do when Mr. Flint returned. He did not want the friendly jeweler to think that he had been dishonest.

It was clear that he was the victim of a conspiracy and that the plot had been engineered by Simon Rich and carried out by his nephew.

As Andy's board was paid by Walter Gale, he would not be distressed by want of employment, but would be able to remain in New York. He might obtain another position, though he foresaw that it would be useless to apply to Simon Rich for a letter of recommendation.

He had not gone more than a hundred feet when he met a boy whom he knew named James Callahan.

"How do you happen to be here, Andy?" he asked. "Are you on an errand for the firm?"

"I have left them."

"Why is that?"

"They -- or rather the clerk -- charged me with stealing a gold watch and pawning it."

"Where?" asked the boy in some excitement.

Andy pointed out the pawnbroker's shop from which he had just come.

"I saw John Crandall coming out of there yesterday."

"You did?"

"Yes."

"I am not surprised. The pawnbroker described to me the boy who pawned the watch, and I recognized John from the description."

"What does it all mean?"

"Mr. Flint has gone out West, and Mr. Rich and John have conspired to get me into trouble."

"When were you discharged?"

"Less than an hour ago."

"Who has taken your place?"

"John Crandall."

James Callahan whistled.

"I see," he said. "It was thundering mean. What are you going to do about it?"

"Wait till Mr. Flint comes home. Give me your address. I may want to call you as a witness."

Callahan gave his number on Ninth Avenue.

"I will note it down."

"How are you going to get along while you are without a place?" asked James with friendly solicitude.

"I have a friend who will pay my board."

"Good! I am glad to hear it."

"Now," thought Andy, "I have a chain of proof that will clear me with Mr. Flint. That is what I care most about."

CHAPTER XX

AN INVITATION TO DINNER

Andy reached his boarding house at four o'clock.

"What brings you home so early, Mr. Grant?" asked Warren, whose door was open. "Is business poor?"

"It is with me," answered Andy. "I am discharged."

"You don't tell me so! How did it happen?"

"My employer is out West, and the head salesman has discharged me and engaged his nephew in my place."

"It's a shame. What shall you do about it?"

"Wait till Mr. Flint gets home."

"I hope you won't leave us."

"No, I think not."

"Of course you will miss your salary. I wish I could lend you some money, but I have not heard from the article I sent to the Century. If accepted, they will send me a large check."

"Thank you, Mr. Warren. I shall be able to get along for the present."

Soon Sam Perkins arrived with a new and gorgeous necktie.

"Glad to see you, Andy," he said. "Won't you go with me to the Star Theater this evening?"

"I can't, Sam. I have no money to spare."

"I thought you got a good salary?"

"Just at present I have none at all. I have been discharged."

"I am sorry for that. I wish there was a vacancy in our place. I should like to get you in there."

"Thank you. That is quite friendly."

Andy was about to go down to supper when Eva, the servant, came upstairs.

"There's a messenger boy downstairs wants to see you, Mr. Grant," she said.

In some surprise Andy went downstairs to see the messenger. He was a short boy of fourteen, Tom Keegan by name.

"I have a letter for Andrew Grant," he said.

"Give it to me. I am Andrew Grant. Here's a dime."

"Thank you," said the boy in a tone of satisfaction, for his weekly income was small.

Andy opened the letter. It was written on fashionable note paper. At the top of the paper was a monogram formed of the letters H and M.

Here is the letter:

MY DEAR MR. GRANT:

I shall be glad to have you take dinner with me at seven o'clock. I should have given you earlier notice, but supposed you would not be back from the store till six o'clock. You will meet my son Roy, who is a year or two younger than yourself, and my brother, John Crawford. Both will be glad to see you.

Yours sincerely,

HENRIETTA MASON.

"What is it, Andy?" asked Sam.

"You can read the note."

"By George, Andy, you are getting into fashionable society! Couldn't you take me along, too?"

"I am afraid I am not well enough acquainted to take such a liberty."

"I'll tell you what I'll do for you. I'll lend you my best necktie."

Sam produced a gorgeous red tie, which he held up admiringly.

"Thank you, Sam," said Andy, "but I think that won't suit me as well as you."

"What are you going to wear?"

Andy took from the bureau drawer a plain black tie.

"That!" exclaimed Sam disgusted. "That is awfully plain."

"It suits my taste."

"Excuse me, Andy, but I don't think you've got any taste."

Andy laughed good-naturedly.

"Certainly my taste differs from yours," he said.

"I suppose you'll have a fine layout. I'd like to go to a fashionable dinner myself."

"I'll tell you all about it when I get back."

"Just mention that you've got a friend -- a stylish young man whom they'd like to meet. That may bring me an invitation next time."

Andy laughed.

"So far as I am concerned, Sam," he said, "I wish you were going. But you have an engagement at the Star Theater."

"So I have. I almost forgot."

Andy had very little time for preparation but made what haste he could, and just as the public clocks struck seven he rang the bell of Mrs. Mason's house.

"I am glad you received my invitation in time," said the lady.

"So am I," returned Andy. "Nothing could have been more welcome."

Just then Roy and her brother, Mr. Crawford, entered.

Roy was a very pleasant-looking boy with dark-brown hair and a dark complexion. He was perhaps two inches shorter than Andy.

"This is Roy," said Mrs. Mason.

"I am glad to see you," said Roy offering his hand.

Andy felt that he should like his new friend.

Next he was introduced to Mr. Crawford, a stout gentleman of perhaps forty, looking very much like his sister.

"I have heard my sister speak of you so often that I am glad to meet you, Andy," he said affably.

"Thank you, sir."

"John, lead the way to the dining room," said his sister.

So they filed downstairs, and took their seats at the table.

Mr. Crawford sat at the head, opposite his sister, while Roy and Andy occupied the sides.

When dinner was nearly over, Mr. Crawford remarked, "I believe, Andy, you are in the employ of Mr. Flint, the jeweler."

"I was," answered Andy.

"Surely you have not left him?" exclaimed Mrs. Mason.

"No, I have been discharged."

"I am surprised to hear it. I thought you were a favorite with Mr. Flint."

"So I was. He does not know I have been discharged."

"You puzzle me."

"Mr. Flint is in Colorado, and Mr. Rich, his head salesman, has taken the opportunity to discharge me and put his nephew in my place."

"But surely he would not venture to do this without some pretext."

"He claims that I took a watch from the case and pawned it."

"Of course that is untrue."

"Yes, and I am in a position to prove it when Mr. Flint returns."

Andy told the story of his visit to the pawn shop and the discovery he made there.

"This is a shameful plot!" said Mrs. Mason indignantly. "I am afraid you are in trouble, deprived of your income."

"Fortunately I have no board to pay. That is paid by the gentleman who procured me the situation."

Presently they went upstairs.

"Roy," said his mother, "we will excuse you for an hour while you are getting your Latin lesson."

"I don't like Latin, mother," grumbled Roy, "at least not tonight. I am afraid I can't fix my thoughts on the lesson. I want to be with Andy."

"What are you studying in Latin, Roy?" asked Andy.

"Caesar."

"If you wish, I will help you."

"Can you?" asked Roy joyfully.

"I have been through Caesar, and Virgil, also. When I left the academy I was studying Cicero."

"Roy will be glad to have your help, Andy," said his mother. "I did not know you were such a scholar."

"I was getting ready for college, but my father's losses required me to break off."

Andy proved such an efficient helper that Roy found himself at leisure in half an hour.

In the meantime Mrs. Mason asked her brother, "What do you think of my protege?"

"He seems a mature and responsible boy."

"Can't you find something for him to do?"

"I will talk with him presently and then decide."

CHAPTER XXI

NEW PROSPECTS

After Roy, with Andy's assistance, had prepared his lesson in Caesar, John Crawford began to converse with him with a view of forming a judgment of his business qualifications.

"Are you especially interested in the jewelry line?" he asked.

"No, sir. It was merely chance that led me to Mr. Flint's store."

"I see you are a Latin scholar. What career did you expect to follow if your father's misfortune had not interrupted your education?"

"I don't think I should care for a profession. I prefer a life of business."

"You have had no special business in view?"

"No, sir. I think I could adapt myself to any that I had an opportunity to follow."

"What pay did you receive from Mr. Flint?"

"Five dollars a week."

"I will tell you why I am inquiring. I am in the real estate business, in rather a large way. I have a boy in the office who is not suited to his position. He is a good scholar, but has no head for business. I have made up my mind to discharge him on Saturday. Would you like his place?"

"Very much, sir."

"I can only offer you five dollars a week, but as soon as you make yourself worth more I will give you a raise."

"That is quite satisfactory, Mr. Crawford. As soon as Mr. Flint returns I can get a recommendation from him. I am quite sure I shall like your business better."

"My sister's recommendation is sufficient."

"Thank you, John," said Mrs. Mason.

"If you become interested in the business and show an aptitude for it, there will be a chance to rise in the firm. It depends upon that. If you only work for the money, you won't rise."

"I understand, Mr. Crawford, and I am satisfied."

"Mother," said Roy, "I wish you would engage Andy to come here evenings and help me with my lessons. I should learn twice as fast. Besides, I should like his company."

Roy was an only child, and it was the desire of his mother's heart that he should acquire a good education. Her means were ample and her disposition generous.

"I don't know but Andy would feel too tired, after being in your uncle's office all day, to teach you in the evening, she said.

"Would you, Andy?" asked Roy.

"No. I should enjoy reviewing my old studies with you."

"Then, I will engage you," said Mrs. Mason. "You can come here at eight every evening."

"I will do so with pleasure."

"And for compensation I will pay you as much as my brother does."

"I wouldn't charge anything for helping Roy," said Andy. "It would only be a pleasure to me."

"Andrew," said Mr. Crawford. "I am afraid you will never become a businessman if you are willing to work on those terms. My advice to you is to accept my sister's offer. She can afford to pay you what she offers, and you have your living to make."

"I shall insist upon paying," said Mrs. Mason, "though I appreciate Andy's generous offer."

"Thank you very much. With such an income I shall feel rich."

"I am so glad you are going to help me, Andy," said Roy. "We'll have bully times."

"I don't think Julius Caesar ever made use of such an expression, Roy," said his uncle.

"When do you wish me to come down to business, Mr. Crawford?" asked Andy.

"You may as well come tomorrow and get broken in before your regular engagement commences."

"I shall be glad to do so."

"For this week you need only stay till three o'clock in the afternoon. There isn't much doing after that."

When Andy went home it will not be wondered at if he was in a state of exhilaration. His discharge from the jeweler's had turned out to his advantage. His income was now ten dollars a week, and he had no board to pay. He certainly ought to lay up money.

He said to himself that now he would not go back to Mr. Flint's even if he had the chance.

When he entered his room he found Sam Perkins waiting for him.

"I have been thinking, Andy," he said, "that I might be able to get you into our store. I will speak to Mr. Chambers tomorrow."

"There is no need, Sam, though I thank you for your kind offer. I have a place."

"What, already?" asked Sam in amazement. "What chance have you had to hunt up a place?"

"The place hunted me up," answered Andy, with a smile. "I met a gentleman at dinner who offered to take me into his employment."

"What business?"

"Real estate."

"What is the firm?"

"John Crawford & Co."

"I know of the house. The office is on lower Broadway. It is a big firm."

"I am glad of that."

"How much are you to get?"

"Five dollars a week."

"Won't you find it hard to live on that?"

"I have got another place, too."

"What do you mean?"

"I am to help a boy with his Latin in the evening. I shall get five dollars a week for that, too."

"What! Ten dollars a week in all?"

"You are right. I give you credit for your mathematical talent."

"Why, Andy, you are born to good luck! I wish I was paid ten dollars a week," said Sam rather enviously. "But I didn't know you understood Latin."

"You don't know how learned I am," said Andy smiling.

"When will you get time for your pupil?"

"In the evening."

"I am sorry for that. I sha'n't often meet you if you are to be occupied day and evening, too."

"We shall meet at breakfast and supper. I sha'n't leave here to go uptown till half-past seven."

"But you can't go to the theater."

"I am willing to give that up for five dollars a week."

"So would I be."

"If I hear of any other boy who needs a Latin tutor I will recommend you."

The next morning Andy reported at Mr. Crawford's office. The office he found to be a large one, consisting of three rooms, one of them small and appropriated to Mr. Crawford's special use.

In the outer rooms were two or three clerks and a boy. The last, James Grey, was a good-natured looking fellow, but he had no force or efficiency. He had already received notice that he was to be discharged on the coming Saturday.

"I suppose you are coming in my place," said he to Andy.
"I suppose so. I am sorry that I shall be throwing you out of a position."

"Oh, you needn't mind. I am to be telephone boy at an uptown hotel. My cousin got the place for me."

"I am glad of that."

"It will be a soft snap, I think."

"What are the hours?"

"I go on at five o'clock in the afternoon, and stay till midnight."

"Will you like that?"

"Oh, well, I can lie abed the next morning till ten or eleven o'clock, and I won't have much to do when I am on duty. I shall buy a lot of dime novels, and that will fill up the time."

"How do you like the real estate business?"

"Oh, so-so. I guess I'll like being a telephone boy better."

"Andrew, you may go round with James, and he will give you a little idea of your duties," said Mr. Crawford. "James, you can go to the post office now."

"All right, sir."

"I hope you will soon get another place."

"I have got one already, sir."

"Indeed! I am very glad."

"I am to be a telephone boy."

"I wish you success."

As they walked to the post office together, James remarked, "Mr. Crawford is a nice man, but I guess I don't hustle enough for him."

"I think I can hustle," said Andy.

"Then you'll suit him."

On Saturday night, when James was paid his salary, he received five dollars extra as a present. Andy thought this very kind and considerate on the part of his new employer. To his surprise he, too, was paid half a week's salary -- something he did not expect.

CHAPTER XXII

JOHN CRANDALL SEEKS TO

INJURE ANDY

Though Simon Rich had succeeded in reinstating his nephew in the store in place of Andy, he was not altogether happy. John Crandall was naturally lazy and inefficient, and his temporary discharge did not seem to have improved him.

When sent out on errands he loitered and had more than once put his uncle to considerable inconvenience. He was obliged to admit to himself that Andy had been more satisfactory.

In the midst of this experience John preferred a request to have his salary raised a dollar a week.

"You know very well that I have no authority to raise your wages," said his uncle sharply.

"Why not, Uncle Simon? You have taken me back on your own authority."

"And I begin to think that I have made a great mistake."

"Perhaps you'd like to have the country boy back again?"

"I am not sure but I would. He did not stay away so long on errands as you do."

"I wonder what he is doing?" said John, starting off on a new tack. "I don't suppose he can get a new place."

"If you see him, you might ask him to call," said Simon Rich.

"Why?" asked John suspiciously.

"I may discharge you and take him back."

"In that case, I will tell Mr. Flint about pawning the watch."

Simon Rich looked at his nephew with anger, mingled with dismay. He began to see, now, that to a certain extent he had put himself in John's power.

"You treacherous young rascal, I have a great mind to wring your neck!" he said wrathfully.

"Uncle Simon," observed John significantly, "I guess you'd better not act hastily."

"What a fool I was to put myself in the power of that cub!" soliloquized the head salesman.

John saw the effect of his words and decided to follow them up.

"Don't you think you can raise my wages?" he asked.

"No, I don't. You will be lucky if you stay here till Mr. Flint comes back. After that, I can't protect you. He will probably be angry to see you back here. I shall have to tell him that I took you in temporarily. Now I will give you some advice. If you want to remain here permanently, turn over a new leaf and work faithfully. In that case I can speak well of you, and Mr. Flint may be induced to retain you."

John began to think that this might be good advice, and for a day or two paid more attention to his duties.

"I wonder I don't see Andy somewhere," he said to himself.

"I am out a good deal, and I ought to meet him. He is probably hunting up positions."

It was not till Tuesday afternoon that he did see him. Andy had been sent to the St. Denis Hotel to meet a customer of the firm. As he came out he fell in with John.

John was the first to see him.

"Hello, Andy!" he exclaimed. "How are you getting along?"

"Pretty well, thank you."

"I suppose you haven't struck a job yet?"

"Oh, yes, I have."

"You have!" exclaimed John in surprise. "What kind of a job?"

"I am in a large real estate office downtown."

"Did they take you without a recommendation?"

"No."

"My uncle wouldn't give you one."

"I wouldn't ask him for one."

"Who did recommend you, then?"

"Mrs. Mason, of West Fifty-Sixth Street."

"I know. She is one of our customers."

"Yes."

"Probably she hasn't heard of your being suspected of pawning a watch from our stock."

"You might tell her."

"Perhaps I shall," John said to himself. "What pay do you get?"

"Five dollars a week."

"I didn't think you would get a place."

Andy smiled.

"I presume Mr. Rich did not care to have me get another place."

"He thought you would have to go back to the country."

"I am better off than when I was in the jewelry store," said Andy. "How are you getting along?"

"Oh, first-class."

"I hope you will be able to keep the place."

"I didn't know but you might be wanting to come back."

"I wouldn't go back if I had the chance."

John was pleased to hear this. He was afraid that Mr. Flint might not be satisfied with his uncle's explanation and that somehow the truth might come out.

"You must excuse me now," said Andy. "I ought to go back to the office at once."

John returned to the jeweler's full of excitement.

"Whom do you think I met just now, Uncle Simon?" he asked.

"Andy?"

"Yes."

"Did you speak with him?"

"Yes."

"I suppose he is hunting for a place."

"No, he has got one."

"Where is he working?"

"In a real estate office downtown. He is getting five dollars a week."

"I didn't think he could get a place without a recommendation."

"He was recommended by one of our customers -- Mrs. Mason."

"I see. Well, that is lucky for him."

Simon Rich spoke indifferently. He was rather glad that Andy had found a place, as Mr. Flint would be less likely to find fault with his dismissal.

Not so John. He had never forgiven Andy for superseding him, and he felt aggrieved that he had so soon found employment. Thinking it over, there came to him a mean suggestion. He might be able to get Andy discharged from his present place.

As his uncle seemed indifferent and might not approve of his contemplated action, he decided to say nothing about it.

That evening, after supper, he made his way up to West Fifty-Sixth Street and sought out the residence of Mrs. Mason.

He rang the bell.

"Can I see Mrs. Mason?" he asked.

"What name shall I mention?"

"Say it is a boy from Mr. Flint's."

Mrs. Mason received the message in some surprise. What could a boy from Flint's have to say to her?

However, she entered the parlor, where John Crandall was waiting to see her.

"You are from Mr. Flint's?" she asked.

"Yes, ma'am."

"What business can you have with me? I have bought no jewelry lately."

"I know it, Mrs. Mason. It isn't about jewelry I wish to speak."

"What, then?"

"I met, today, a boy who was lately employed by our firm -- Andrew Grant."

"Well?"

"He said you had recommended him to a real estate firm downtown."

"I did so."

"Perhaps you didn't know that he had been discharged from our place for dishonesty."

"I begin to understand," thought Mrs. Mason, and she sat down and examined John curiously.

"Did he steal anything?"

"Yes, ma'am," answered John glibly. "He took a watch -- a gold watch -- out of the case and pawned it."

"That was bad. And you have come up to tell me of it? You are very considerate. Did Mr. Rich send you, or do you come of your own accord?"

"I came of my own accord. I thought you were deceived in the boy."

"What do you think I ought to do?"

"I thought you would take back the recommendation and get the boy discharged."

"Can you wait here half an hour while I consider what is best to be done?"

"Oh, yes, ma'am." ("I guess I've put a spoke in his wheel," thought John.)

In about half an hour the door opened, and to John's amazement Andy walked in.

"You here!" he gasped.

"Yes. I hear you have been warning Mrs. Mason against me."

"I thought she ought to know that you were sent away from our store in disgrace."

"I have something to say to you," said Andy quietly. "I have been to the pawnbroker's and got a description of the boy who pawned the watch!"

John turned pale.

"I see you understand," Andy went on, "who did it. So do I, and so does Mrs. Mason. You won't make anything by your attempt to injure me. Good evening!"

John Crandall left the house without a word. He began to be alarmed.

"Suppose Andy tells Flint," he soliloquized. "No matter; he can't prove it."

But he felt uneasy, nevertheless. He did not say anything to his uncle about his visit.

CHAPTER XXIII

MR. FLINT'S RETURN

Mr. Crawford was something more than an ordinary real estate dealer. He was thorough and painstaking in whatever he undertook.

In his private office he had a library of volumes relating to architecture, practical building, real estate, law, etc. This Andy discovered, and he asked his employer if he might borrow books therefrom.

Mr. Crawford seemed pleased, but he asked, "Do you think you will feel any interest in such dry volumes?"

"I shall not read for interest, but for improvement," answered Andy. "If I am to follow up this business I want to find out all I can about it."

"You are an unusually sensible boy," said Mr. Crawford. "I am sure you will succeed."

"I mean to, if it is possible."

From this time John Crawford felt an added interest in Andy, and he took pains to push him forward and gave him practical information about real estate.

"How do you like Andy, John?" asked Mrs. Mason not long afterward.

"He is a treasure. He does credit to your recommendation."

"I am very much pleased to hear you say so. I consider him a remarkable boy. Roy gets much higher marks at school since Andy began to help him in his lessons."

One day Andy was sent up to the Grand Central Depot on an errand. He arrived just as a train came in from the West. What was his surprise to see Mr. Flint getting out of a parlor car.

"Mr. Flint!" he cried joyfully.

"Andy!" exclaimed the jeweler. "It seems pleasant to see a home face. But how do you happen to be up here at this time? Did Mr. Rich send you?"

"Then you have not heard -- " began Andy.

"Heard what?"

"That I have been discharged from your store."

"When did this happen?" asked the jeweler abruptly.

"About two weeks ago."

"Rich never wrote me about it. Who is in your place?"

"John Crandall."

"His nephew? The boy I discharged?"

"Yes, sir."

Mr. Flint's face assumed a stern look.

"This will have to be explained," he said. "What was the pretext for discharging you?"

"Dishonesty. He charged me with stealing a gold watch and pawning it."

"Ridiculous!"

"Then you don't believe me guilty?"

"Certainly not."

"Thank you, Mr. Flint."

"Tell me the circumstances."

"Please excuse me now, Mr. Flint. I am in a real estate office, and am on an errand. If you like, I will call at your house and explain. In the meantime I will let Mr. Rich give you his version."

"Call this evening, Andy."

"It will have to be between seven and half-past seven, as I have a pupil in the evening."

"Come to supper at my house, as soon after six as possible."

"Very well, sir."

Mr. Flint had telegraphed to Simon Rich of his coming, but through some mistake the telegram did not reach him, so that he was quite taken by surprise when his employer entered the store.

"I had no idea you were anywhere near New York, Mr. Flint," he said.

"Didn't you get my telegram from Buffalo, Mr. Rich?"

"No, sir. I hope you are well."

Just then John Crandall came in from an errand.

"You here!" said the jeweler. "Where is Andy Grant?"

"I was obliged to discharge him," replied Rich nervously.

"Why?"

"Very much to my surprise I discovered that he had stolen a gold watch from the case."

"What evidence had you of it?"

"I found the pawn ticket in his pocket. He pawned it on Third Avenue."

"This surprises me very much," said the jeweler quietly. "Andrew did not strike me as a dishonest boy."

"I was amazed, sir. I could hardly believe my eyes."

"What led you to search for the ticket?"

"I knew that the watch must have been taken either by him or John, who came into the shop occasionally. I accordingly searched both."

"And you found the ticket in Andrew's pocket?"

"Yes, sir."

"What did he say? Did he admit the theft?"

"No. He brazened it out, but of course the evidence was overwhelming."

"So you discharged him?"

"Yes. I did not dare to have him remain."

"And you engaged your nephew in his place?"

"Yes, sir. John happened to be here and knew something of the duties, so I engaged him temporarily, subject, of course, to your approval."

"Where is Andrew now? Have you seen him since?"

"John saw him one day. Where was it, John?"

"On Broadway, near the St. Denis Hotel. He said he had a place."

"Where?"

"In a real estate office."

"I suppose you gave him no recommendation, Mr. Rich?"

"No, sir. I couldn't do it conscientiously. Of course, now that you have returned, if you are dissatisfied with John's being here, we can advertise for another boy."

"I will take a day to consider it. I shall only stay here half an hour and then go up to the house."

When Mr. Flint left the store, Simon Rich said, "The old man took Andy's discharge more quietly than I anticipated."

"Do you think he will let me stay, Uncle Simon?"

"I can't tell yet. One thing I must tell you -- you won't stay long unless you turn over a new leaf and attend to your duties."

"I'll do that, never fear! What I am afraid of is that Andy will come around and tell a lot of lies."

"I don't think it will work. You see, the pawn ticket was found in his pocket. He can't get over that very well."

John knew more than his uncle of the nature of Andy's defense, and he could not help feeling apprehensive.

Soon after six o'clock Andy made his appearance at Mr. Flint's house, where he was cordially received.

"I have heard the story of Mr. Rich, Andy," he said. "Now let me have your defense."

"I can give it very briefly. The watch was pawned by John Crandall. Of course it was given to him by Mr. Rich."

"How did you find that out?"

"I went around to the pawnbroker's and obtained a description of the boy who pawned the watch. It tallied exactly with John's appearance. That was not all. I met, the same day, a boy named Jimmy Callahan. He saw John coming out of the pawnbroker's the day before the charge was made against me."

"That is pretty conclusive. Can you explain how the ticket was put in your pocket?"

"No, sir. That puzzles me."

"It could easily be done, no doubt. Now, do you want to return to my employ?"

"No, sir, I think not. I am in a real estate office, and I think there is more chance for me to rise."

"How did you obtain the position?"

"Through Mrs. Mason, of West Fifty-Sixth Street. She has been a very good friend to me. The gentleman who employs me is her brother."

"I shall be sorry to lose you, Andy, but I wish you to consult your own interest. As to John Crandall, I shall discharge him at once. I will not permit him to profit by the conspiracy against you. Can you stay this evening?"

"No, sir. I am helping Mrs. Mason's son, Roy, in his Latin lessons. For this I am paid five dollars per week."

"You seem to be very well provided for, I must say."

"Yes, sir. I have been fortunate."

The next day Mr. Flint notified Simon Rich that he was acquainted with the manner in which evidence had been procured against Andy. Then he turned to the nephew.

"The watch was pawned by you, John," he said, "under the direction of your uncle."

"No, sir," said John. "If Andy Grant has told you this he has told a lie."

"The matter is easily settled. Come around with me to the pawnbroker's."

John stammered and finally confessed.

"Of course I cannot retain your services after this. You, Mr. Rich, may remain till the end of the month. I shall then feel obliged to make a change."

Never were two conspirators more quickly punished. Simon Rich repented bitterly yielding to the temptation to injure Andy. His malice had recoiled upon himself.

CHAPTER XXIV

ANDY MAKES AN INVESTMENT

Andy wrote to his friend, Walter Gale, -- who, it will be remembered, was watching in Pennsylvania by the bedside of his uncle -- giving him an account of his change of business. He received the following reply:

I felt indignant when I read your news of the conspiracy of Simon Rich but was pleased that it led to your advantage. I am inclined to think that you will find your new business a better one than the jewelry trade. The latter, if you went in for yourself, would call for a large capital. In the real estate business capital is not so much needed as good judgment and a large lot of acquaintances. I am not personally acquainted with Mr. Crawford but know him by reputation as an energetic and honorable businessman. If you do not find your income adequate, all you have to do is to apply to me. I will send you fifty dollars or more at any time.

Now, as to the prospects for my return, they are remote. My uncle seems cheered by my presence, and his health has improved. He cannot live more than a year or two at best, but when I came here it seemed to be only a matter of months. I shall remain while I can do him good.

When Mr. Flint returns he will do you justice. You can afford to wait, as your income is larger than before. You suggest that I need not continue to pay your board. This, however, I intend to do, and I will advise you to lay aside some money every week and deposit in a savings bank. The habit of saving is excellent and cannot be formed too early."

"I am lucky to have such a friend," reflected Andy as he finished reading this letter. "I will try to make myself worthy of such good fortune."

At the end of six months Andy had acquired a large practical acquaintance with the real estate business. He displayed a degree of judgment which surprised Mr. Crawford.

"You seem more like a young man than a boy," he said. "I am not at all sure but I could leave my business in your hands if I wished to be absent."

This compliment pleased Andy. He had also been raised to seven dollars a week, and this he regarded as a practical compliment.

One evening on his return from West Fifty-Sixth Street he strayed into the Fifth Avenue Hotel where he sat down to rest in the reading room.

Two men were sitting near him whose conversation he could not help overhearing.

"I own a considerable plot in Tacoma," said one. "I bought it two years ago when I was on my way back from California. I should like to sell the plot if I could get a purchaser."

"If the Northern Pacific Railroad is ever completed, the land will be valuable," replied the other.

"True, but will it ever be completed? That date will be very remote, I fancy."

"I don't think so. I would buy the land myself if I had the money, but just at present I have none to spare. How much did you invest?"

"A thousand dollars."

"You might sell, perhaps, through a real estate agent?"

"The real estate agents here know very little of Western property. I should not know to whom to apply."

Andy thought he saw a chance to procure business for his firm.

"Gentlemen," he said, "will you excuse my saying that I am in a real estate office, and think you can make some satisfactory arrangement with us?"

At the same time he handed the owner of the Tacoma property a card of the firm.

"Crawford!" repeated his friend. "Yes, that is a reputable firm. You cannot do better than adopt the young man's suggestion."

Andy Grant had written his name on the card.

"You are rather young for a real estate agent, Mr. Grant," remarked the lot owner.

Andy smiled.

"I am only a subordinate," he said.

"Has your principal ever dealt in Western property?" asked Mr. Bristol.

"Not to any extent, but I have heard him speak favorably of it."

"I will call at your office tomorrow before noon, then."

Andy apprised Mr. Crawford of the appointment made.

"I shall be glad to see your acquaintance, Andy," said Mr. Crawford. "I have been advised by a friend of mine in Washington that the railroad is sure to be completed within a short time. This land will be worth buying. Have you any money?"

"I have a hundred dollars in a savings bank," answered Andy.

"Then I will give you a quarter interest in the purchase, and you can give me a note for the balance which at present you are unable to pay. I am sure we shall make a good deal of money within a short time, and I want you to reap some advantage, as it will have come to me through you."

"Thank you, sir. I shall be very glad to have a share in the investment."

About eleven o'clock, James Bristol, who proved to be a resident of Newark, New Jersey, presented himself at the office and was introduced by Andy to Mr. Crawford.

"Andy has told me of your business," said the real estate agent. "You have some property in Tacoma."

"Yes. I was persuaded to invest in it some two years ago. Now I need the money. Do you think you can find me a customer?"

"What do you ask for it?"

"A thousand dollars -- the same price I paid."

"Is it eligibly situated?"

"If the town ever amounts to anything, it will be in the business part."

"How many lots will it divide into?"

"Twenty-five of the usual city dimensions."

"Then I think I will take it off your hands. One part I will reserve for myself, and the other part I will allot to a friend."

"Can you pay me cash?"

"Yes. I will make out a check at once."

Mr. Bristol breathed a sigh of satisfaction.

"I don't mind telling you," he said, "that I am very glad to realize on the investment. I have to meet a note for five hundred dollars in three days, and I was at a loss to know how to raise the money."

"Then the transaction will be mutually satisfactory," rejoined Mr. Crawford.

"Well, Andy," said his employer, when his customer left the office, "we are now Western land owners. I will draw up a note, which I will get you to sign, for a hundred and fifty dollars, and you can assign to me the money in the savings bank. I shall expect interest at the rate of six per cent."

"I shall be very glad to pay it, sir."

It was a satisfaction to Andy to think that he had made an investment which was likely in many years to make him golden returns. He began to read with interest the accounts of the growth and development of the West and decided to be unusually economical in the future, so as to be able to pay up the note due to Mr. Crawford and so he might feel that he owned his Western property without encumbrance.

While Andy, as a rule, dressed neatly, there was one respect in which he did not win the approval of his neighbor, Sam Perkins.

"I should think a boy with your income would be more particular about his neckties," said Sam.

"What's the matter with my neckties, Sam? Are they not neat?"

"Yes, but they are plain, such as a Quaker might wear. Why don't you get a showy tie, like mine?"

Andy smiled as he noticed the gorgeous tie which his friend wore.

"I don't like to be showy," he said.

"You'll never attract the attention of the girls with such a plain tie as you wear. Now, when I walked on Fifth Avenue last Sunday afternoon, as many as twenty girls looked admiringly at my tie."

"That would make me feel bashful, Sam."

"Let me bring you one from the store like mine. You shall have it at the wholesale price."

"No, I think not. It wouldn't be as becoming to me as to you. I don't want to be considered a dude."

"I don't mind it. Next week I'm going to buy a pair of patent leathers. They will be really economical, as I shall not have to spend money on shines."

One Saturday afternoon, when Andy was walking through one of the quiet streets west of Bleecker, his attention was drawn to a small boy, apparently about eleven years old, who was quietly crying as he walked along the sidewalk. He had never seen the boy before that he could remember, yet his face wore a familiar expression.

CHAPTER XXV

SQUIRE CARTER'S RELATIVES

Andy was kind-hearted, and the boy's evident sorrow appealed to him. He went forward and placed his hand on the boy's shoulder.

"What is the matter?" he asked.

"I went to the baker's to buy some bread for mother, and the baker tells me that the quarter is a bad one."

"Let me look at it."

The coin had a dull appearance and a greasy feeling. It was unquestionably counterfeit.

"Yes, it is bad," said Andy. "Is your mother poor?"

"Very poor," answered the boy. "This quarter was all the money she had, and now we shall have no supper."

"Whom do you mean by 'we'?"

"My little brother and myself."

Andy intended at first simply to give the boy a good coin for the bad one, but he saw that there was a call for something more.

"Do you live near here?" he asked.

"Yes, sir. Just across the street."

"I will go back with you to the baker's, and then I will go with you to see your mother. Perhaps I can help her."

The boy put his hand confidingly in Andy's, and the two went a little distance to the baker's.

"Now make your purchases," said Andy.

"If you have brought back that bad quarter I won't take it," announced the baker sharply.

"I will pay you," said Andy quietly.

"Then it's all right. The boy brought me a very bad quarter. I have to look sharp, for a good many bad coins are offered me."

Andy produced a genuine silver piece, and the bread was handed to the boy, with the change.

The boy looked at it hesitatingly.

"It is yours," he said to Andy.

"No, I have changed quarters with you. I will keep the bad one." Again he looked at the boy, and again the resemblance to some familiar face puzzled him.

"What is your name?" he asked.

"Ben Carter."

Carter! That explained it. The boy looked like Conrad Carter, though he had a pleasanter expression.

"Have you an Uncle Philemon?" he inquired.

"How did you know?" asked the boy in surprise.

"Because you look like Conrad Carter."

"He is my cousin."

"And you are poor?"

"Yes."

"Your uncle is considered rich."

"I know he is, but he won't do anything for mother."

Andy was now all the more desirous of seeing the boy's family.

"I know your uncle," he said. "Do you think he knows you are so poor?"

"Yes, for mother has written to him."

By this time they had reached the place which Ben called home.

"Go upstairs and I will follow," said Andy.

They went up two flights, and the boy opened a door at the top of the landing.

There was a woman not far from forty in the room. On her face was a look of settled sorrow. At her knee was a small boy five years of age. She looked at Andy inquiringly.

"Mother," said Ben, "here is the bread. I couldn't have bought it, for the quarter was bad, if this boy had not given me another quarter."

"This young gentleman," corrected the mother.

"No, Mrs. Carter. I am a boy, and I prefer to be called so. I came up with Ben, for I find that he is related to Squire Carter, of Arden, whom I know very well."

"You know Philemon Carter?"

"Yes, he lives in Arden. That is my birthplace."

Mrs. Carter's countenance fell.

"Philemon Carter was my husband's brother," she said, "but there is little friendship between us."

"He is reputed rich."

"And we are poor. I see you wonder at that. When my husband's father died, Philemon was executor. It was understood that he was worth twenty-five thousand dollars. Yet of this amount my poor husband received but one thousand. I may be uncharitable, but I have always felt that Philemon cheated us out of our rightful share."

"I should not be surprised. I never liked Squire Carter. He always seemed to me to be a selfish man."

"He has certainly acted selfishly toward us."

"Does he know of your poverty?"

"Yes. Only two weeks ago, in a fit of despair, I wrote to him for help. Here is his answer."

She handed a letter to Andy. He instantly recognized the handwriting of the magnate of Arden.

"Shall I read it?" he asked.

"Yes, do so, and let me know what you think of it."

This was the letter:

SOPHIA:

I have received your letter and am surprised that you should expect me to help support you. You are my brother's widow, it is true, but your destitution is no fault of mine. My brother was always shiftless and unpractical, and to such men good luck never comes. He might at any rate have insured his life and so made comfortable provision for you. You cannot expect me to repair his negligence. You say you have two boys, one eleven years of age. He is certainly able to earn money by selling papers or tending an office.

As for myself, I am not a rich man, but have always been careful to meet my expenses and provide for the future. I, too, have a son, Conrad, whom I think it my duty to educate and start in life. Any money I might send you would be so much taken from him. I advise you to apply to some charitable society if you need temporary assistance. It will be much better than to write me begging letters.

Yours truly,

PHILEMON CARTER.

"This is a very cold-blooded letter," said Andy indignantly. "He might at least have enclosed a five-dollar bill."

"He enclosed nothing. I shall never apply to him again."

"Philemon Carter is considered to be one of the richest men in Arden. He is taxed for twenty-five thousand dollars and is probably worth double that sum. People wonder where he got all his money."

"A part of it is my husband's rightful share of the estate, I have no doubt."

"Can you do nothing about it?"

"How can I? I am poor and have no influential friends. He denies everything."

"I will think of that, Mrs. Carter. I know a lawyer downtown who may some time look into the matter for you. In the meanwhile, is there any special work you can do?"

"Before I was married I was, for a time, a typist."

"I will see if I can hear of a situation of that kind. The lawyer I spoke of may require an operator."

"I would thankfully accept such a position."

"Does Ben earn anything?"

"He makes a little selling papers."

"He ought to be going to school at his age."

"If I could get any work to do I would send him."

"Mrs. Carter, will you accept a little help from me?"

Andy drew a five-dollar bill from his wallet and tendered it to the widow.

"But," she said, "can you spare this? It is a large sum, and you are only a boy, probably not earning much."

"I am a boy, but I am handsomely paid for my services. Besides, I have good friends to whom I can apply if I run short of money."

"Heaven bless you!" said Mrs. Carter earnestly. "You cannot tell how much good this money will do me. This morning I was utterly discouraged. I felt that the Lord had forsaken me. But I was mistaken. He has raised up for me a good friend, who -- "

"Hopes to be of a good deal more service to you. I must leave you now, but I shall bear you in mind, and hope soon to be the bearer of good tidings. I will take down your address and call upon you again soon. Will you allow me to offer you a suggestion?"

"Certainly."

"Then send out and buy some meat. This dry bread is not sufficient for you. Don't be afraid to spend the money I leave with you. I will see that you have more."

As Andy left Mrs. Carter's humble home he felt more than ever the cold and selfish character of the man who, himself living luxuriously, suffered his brother's family to want.

CHAPTER XXVI

MR. WARREN AND HIS SUCCESS

Andy told Mr. Crawford about the poor family he had visited and what he had done to help them.

"You must let me refund the money, Andy," said his employer. "Five dollars is a good deal for a boy to give."

"Don't forget that I have a double income, Mr. Crawford. I would prefer that this money should come from me. If you are willing to give another five dollars, it will be appreciated."

"Then I will make it ten. Will you take charge of this bill and give it to Mrs. Carter?"

"With the greatest pleasure, Mr. Crawford. You have no idea what happiness it will give the family."

"I am glad you called my attention to their needs. If I could do anything more to help them -- "

"You can if you know any one who wants a typist."

"Is the boy able to work a typewriter?"

"No, but the mother is. Before her marriage she was in a lawyer's office."

"That is a fortunate suggestion. I have a college friend -- a classmate at Columbia -- Mr. Gardner, who has just parted with his typist, who is about to be married."

"May I call at his office and ask for the job for Mrs. Carter?"

"Yes. It is on Nassau Street."

Andy seized his hat and went over to the lawyer's office.

It was 132 Nassau Street in the Vanderbilt Building. He went up in the elevator and found Mr. Gardner in.

"I come from Mr. Crawford," said Andy. "He says you need a typist."

"Are you a typist?"

"No. I ask for the position for a lady," and he told the story.

"You say she has had experience in a lawyer's office?"

"Yes, sir."

"That will make her more desirable. When can she call?"

"I will have her here tomorrow morning at any hour."

"Say ten o'clock -- a little before, perhaps."

The lawyer was a pleasant-looking man of medium age, and Andy felt sure that he would be a kind and considerate employer.

After office hours and before going up to his pupil, Andy called at the humble home of Mrs. Carter. The widow's face brightened as she saw him.

"You are my good friend," she said. "You are welcome."

"My employer, Mr. Crawford, sends you this," and Andy displayed the bill.

"It is a godsend. It will enable me to pay my rent, due on Saturday, and give me three dollars over."

"But that is not all. I have procured you a job as typewriter in a lawyer's office. You will have to be on hand tomorrow morning a little before ten. The office is Mr. Gardner's at 132 Nassau Street."

"I can hardly believe in my good fortune. I will be there."

"Can you leave the children?"

"I will ask my neighbor, Mrs. Parker, to look after them. What a good young man you are!" she exclaimed gratefully.

"Not young man -- boy," corrected Andy with a smile.

"Won't you stay and take a cup of tea?"

"Thank you, Mrs. Carter, but I have an evening engagement. Oh, by the way, I forgot to say that Mr. Gardner will pay you ten dollars a week."

"I shall feel rich. I shall no longer be worried by thoughts of starvation."

"Some time you might consult Mr. Gardner about your brother-in-law's withholding your share of the estate. He will be able to advise you."

Andy felt a warm glow in his heart at the thought of the happiness he had been instrumental in bringing to the poor family. He had learned the great lesson that some never learn -- that there is nothing so satisfactory as helping others. We should have a much better world if that was generally understood.

The next day Andy received a letter from his good friend, Valentine Burns. He read it eagerly, for it brought him some home news, and in spite of his success he had not forgotten Arden and his many friends there.

This was the letter:

DEAR ANDY:

How long it seems since I saw you! You know that you were my best friend, and of course I miss you very much. To be sure, there is Conrad, who seems willing to bestow his company upon me, as my father happens to be pretty well off, but I look upon Conrad as a snob and don't care much about him. When we met yesterday, he inquired after you.

'What's your friend, Andy Grant, doing in the city?'

'He is in a real estate office,' I replied.

'Humph! how much does he get paid?'

'Five dollars.'

'That is probably more than he earns, but it isn't much to live on.'

I didn't care to tell him that you had another income, but said, 'Don't you think you could live on it?'

'I couldn't live on ten dollars a week,' said Conrad loftily. 'But, then, I haven't been accustomed to live like Andy Grant.'

It must be pleasant for you to know that Conrad feels so much interest in your welfare.

Sometimes I see your father. He looks careworn. I suppose he is thinking of the difficult position in which he is placed. I am sorry to say that last week he lost his best cow by some disease. I heard that he valued it at fifty dollars. I hope that you won't let this worry you. The tide will turn some time. I saw your mother day before yesterday. She is glad of your success, but of course she misses you. She always receives me very cordially, knowing that we are close friends.

I wish I could see you, Andy. You have no idea how I miss you. I like quite a number of the boys, but none is so near to me as you were.

Well, Andy, I must close. Come to Arden soon, if you can. It will do us good to see you, and I think even Conrad will be glad as it will give him a chance to pump you as to your position.

Your affectionate friend,

VALENTINE BURNS.

"So father has lost his best cow -- old Whitey," said Andy thoughtfully. "If I were not owing money to Mr. Crawford for the land in Tacoma I would buy him a new one, but in time I hope the land will be valuable, and then I can make the loss good to father."

Andy's father lost his best cow

The reader has not, I hope, forgotten Andy's fellow lodger, S. Byron Warren. Mr. Warren was always writing something for the Century, the Atlantic, or some other leading magazine but never had been cheered by an acceptance. The magazine editors seemed leagued against him.

But one evening, when Andy returned from the office, he found Mr. Warren beaming with complacence.

"You look happy tonight, Mr. Warren," he said.

"Yes," answered the author. "Look at that."

He held out to Andy an eight-page paper called The Weekly Magnet and pointed out a story of two columns on the second page. Under the title Andy read, "By S. Byron Warren." It was called "The Magician's Spell; A Tale of Sunny Spain."

"I congratulate you," said Andy. "When did you write the story?"

"Last winter."

"How does it happen to be published so late?"

"You see, I sent it first to Scribner's, then to Harper's, and then to the Atlantic. They didn't seem to fancy it, so I sent it to the Magnet."

"I hope they paid you for it."

"Yes," answered Warren proudly. "They gave me a dollar and a half for it."

"Isn't that rather small?"

"Well, it is small, but the paper is poor. The editor wrote to me that he would be glad to pay me ten dollars for such a sketch when they are more prosperous."

"I suppose you will write again? You must feel greatly encouraged."

"I have been writing another story today. I shall mail it to them tomorrow."

"I hope the Magnet will prosper for your sake."

"Thank you. I hope so, too. Ah, Andy, you don't know how it seems to see your own words in print!" said the author.

"I am afraid I never shall, Mr. Warren. I was not intended for an author."

"Oh, I think you might write something," said Warren patronizingly.

"No. I shall leave the literary field to you."

CHAPTER XXVII

ANDY MAKES A COMMISSION

Mr. Crawford was busy in his office when a gentleman of fifty entered.

"I hope you are at leisure, Crawford," he said.

"But I am not, Mr. Grayling. I am unusually busy."

"I wanted you to go out and show me that house in Mount Vernon which you mentioned to me the other day. My wife is desirous of moving from the city for the sake of the children."

"Won't tomorrow do?"

"Tomorrow I shall be busy myself. Today is so fine that I managed to get off. Can't you manage to go?"

"No, Grayling, I can't possibly be spared from the office."

"Is there no one you can send with me?"

Mr. Crawford hesitated a moment. Then, as his eye fell upon Andy, he had a sudden thought.

"I will send this young man," he said.

Mr. Grayling smiled.

"He seems quite a young man," he said.

"Yes," said Mr. Crawford, with an answering smile, "he is several years short of forty."

"If you think he will do I shall be glad of his company."

"Wait five minutes, and I will give him the necessary instructions."

"Have you ever been in Mount Vernon, Andy?" asked his employer.

"Yes, sir. I have a friend there, and I once spent a Sunday there."

"Mr. Grayling wishes to purchase a residence there. I shall place him in your charge and give you an order for the key. I will mention some points to which I wish you to call his attention."

Andy was pleased with the commission. It seemed like a step in advance.

"Thank you, Mr. Crawford, for your confidence in me."

"If you succeed in selling the house to Mr. Grayling, I will give you one per cent commission."

"I will do my best, sir. I have no claim to anything except through your kindness."

"Now let me see how much business ability you have."

Andy and the prospective purchaser took the cars at the Grand Central Station, and in forty minutes found themselves in Mount Vernon.

At the depot, much to his satisfaction, Andy found his friend, Tom Blake.

What brings you here, Andy?" asked Tom in surprise.

"I have come to show the Griffith house to this gentleman. Can you direct me to it?"

"I will go with you."

"Thank you, Tom. You will be doing me a favor. Is it far?"

"Little more than half a mile."

"Shall we walk or ride, Mr. Grayling?"

"Walk, by all means. It is a charming day, and a walk will do me good."

They reached the house. It was a spacious country residence in good condition, and Mr. Grayling was favorably impressed. The key was procured and they entered.

The interior bore out the promise of the exterior. The rooms were well and even handsomely finished. They were twelve in number, and there was a good-sized bathroom.

"I wonder if the plumbing is good?" said Mr. Grayling.

"I will test it as far as I can," said Andy.

"You seem to have a good deal of experience for one so young."

"No, sir, not very much, but I have made a careful study of the subject. Mr. Crawford has a good architectural library, and I have made use of it."

After a careful inspection, Andy made a favorable report.

"Of course," he said, "if I am mistaken we will make matters right."

"That will be satisfactory. What is your price for the house?"

"Eight thousand dollars."

A spacious and furnished room in the country house

Mr. Grayling, after a brief consideration, said, "That seems reasonable. I will buy the house. How soon can you give me possession?"

"In a week."

"Very good. Then our business seems to be concluded. We will catch the next train back to the city."

"Would you mind giving me a memorandum stating that you will buy the house?"

"I will do so. We will stop at a stationery store, and I will make it out."

When Andy re-entered Mr. Crawford's office the real estate agent inquired, "How does Mr. Grayling like the house?"

"He has bought it."

"Is it possible? At what figure?"

"Eight thousand dollars."

"Good! I was authorized to take two hundred dollars less, if need be."

"He asked no reduction."

"I hope he won't change his mind."

"He won't. Here is his written agreement to take the house."

"Excellent. Did he offer this assurance?"

"No, sir. I asked for it."

"Andy, you have succeeded admirably. I shall have great pleasure in keeping my promise and paying you eighty dollars, or one per cent, on the purchase money."

"That will be very acceptable, Mr. Crawford. I don't often earn eighty dollars in one day."

In reply to Mr. Crawford's inquiries, Andy gave a detailed account of his visit, and his employer drew a check for eighty dollars which he placed in his hands.

"Now that I see what you can do," he said, "I shall send you out again."

"Perhaps you will find my services too expensive."

"No. In addition to my regular percentage I receive an extra hundred dollars for getting the full eight thousand dollars."

Andy cashed the check and deposited the money in a savings bank. He did not pay it to Mr. Crawford on account of the land in Tacoma, for it occurred to him that he might have occasion to use it.

In this he proved correct.

Three weeks later he received a letter from his father. Sterling Grant was a farmer, little used to writing letters, and Andy knew that there must be some special reason for his writing at this time.

He opened the letter quickly, and this was what he read:

DEAR ANDY:

I am in trouble. Next Tuesday the semi-annual interest on Squire Carter's three thousand dollars falls due, and I have but twenty dollars to meet it. My crops have not been up to the average. I have lost my best cow, and somehow everything seems to have gone against me. I expected to sell ten tons of hay and have had but seven to spare. This alone made a difference of sixty dollars.

I saw the squire yesterday and told him how I was situated. I asked him if he would kindly wait for the greater part of the interest, accepting twenty dollars on account. He at once refused. 'I am sorry you have been unlucky, Mr. Grant,' he said, 'but of course I am not responsible for your misfortune. The three thousand dollars I lent you I regard strictly as an investment. Had I supposed the interest would not be paid promptly, I should, of course, have declined to lend. You will have to meet the interest, or take the consequences.'

I have tried to borrow the money in the village, but thus far I have been unable to do so. I may have to sell two of my cows, but that will cripple me, for, as you know, I depend a good deal on selling milk and butter. Of course this worries me a good deal. I don't know why I write to you, for with your small pay it is hardly likely that you can help me. Still, if you have ten or fifteen dollars to spare, it will aid me. If your friend, Mr. Gale, were near at hand, perhaps he would advance a little money. I might get along with selling one cow, in that case. Two would cripple me.

Let me know at once what you can do so that I may make plans. Your mother is as well as usual except that she is worried. We both send love.

Your affectionate father,

STERLING GRANT.

When Andy read this letter he felt, with a thrill of joy, that he had it in his power to relieve his father from anxiety. He had, with the commission received recently from Mr. Crawford, a hundred and fifty dollars in the bank. He withdrew eighty dollars of this, and then explaining to Mr. Crawford his reason for it, asked for time for a visit home.

"Certainly, Andy," said the real estate agent. "Can I lend you any money?"

"No, sir. I have enough."

As he could not leave till the next day, he telegraphed his father in this way:

Don't worry. I shall be home tomorrow.

ANDY

CHAPTER XXVIII

ANDY'S VISIT HOME

When Andy stepped on the station platform at Arden, he looked about him to see if any of his friends were in sight.

To his great satisfaction he saw Valentine Burns, who had come to escort an aunt to the cars.

"Where did you drop from, Andy?" he asked in surprise.

"From the city. I am going to stop over Sunday."

"Good! I am delighted to see you."

"And I to see you. You are my dearest friend -- except Conrad."

Valentine smiled.

"Of course no one is so near to me as he. Well, what's the news?"

"The only news I know of comes from Conrad. I hope it isn't true."

"What did he say?"

"That your father couldn't pay the interest on the mortgage held by his father and was going to be turned out, though the squire might take your two best cows and call it even."

"He seems to be a good friend of the family, doesn't he?" remarked Andy quietly.

"It isn't true, is it?"

"It is true that father hasn't money enough to pay the interest."

"What will happen, then?"

"You forget that he has a rich son," said Andy with a smile.

"Can you help him out?"

"That is what I am here for."

"I am very glad to hear it," said Valentine with an air of relief. "Even if I didn't like your family, I wouldn't like to see Conrad triumph over you."

"Come around this evening, Val. We shall have plenty to talk about."

"I will."

When Andy entered the farmhouse he received a warm welcome from his mother and a cordial grasp of the hand from his father, who was less demonstrative. But there was an air of grave anxiety on the faces of both.

"I am glad to see you, Andy," said Sterling Grant, "but I wish you had come under more cheerful circumstances. We are in a good deal of trouble."

"I have come to get you out of it."

"Can you?" asked the farmer in surprise.

"Yes. How much have you got toward the interest?"

"Only twenty dollars."

"And the whole sum is -- "

"Ninety dollars."

"I can give you the seventy dollars you require."

"Where did you get the money? Have you borrowed it?"

"No. It belongs to me. I will explain later. Now I am hungry, and while mother is looking for some lunch for me we will talk about other matters."

"I am very much relieved, Andy. I will go and tell the squire I shall be able to meet the interest."

"Don't do it, father. We will leave him to suppose it will not be paid, and see what course he intends to pursue. Don't breathe a word to undeceive him."

I will do as you say, Andy, though I don't know your object. Do you still like your place in New York?"

"Yes. I am learning the business fast and have good hopes for the future. Mr. Crawford is an excellent man, and he takes an interest in me."

"That is good. After all, things are brightening. When I got up this morning I felt about discouraged."

"I telegraphed you not to worry, father."

Meanwhile Mrs. Grant was preparing an appetizing lunch for her son. She knew just what he liked. When it was placed on the table, he did full justice to it.

"It tastes better than anything I get in the city, mother," he said.

"I didn't suppose our plain table would compare with city meals."

"They're not in it with you," said Andy. "I am only afraid I shall make myself sick by overeating."

Mrs. Grant was greatly pleased that Andy had not lost his taste for home fare.

"How you have grown, Andy!" she said. "And you are looking so well, too! Do you have to work very hard?"

"Hard work agrees with me, mother. No, I don't hurt myself."

"I wish I could be here when the squire comes for the interest," Andy said later.

"He will call this evening. You will see him," said Sterling Grant.

"Then I shall be sure to stay at home."

Meanwhile, at the house of Squire Carter, there was a conference between father and son.

Conrad had a new and bright idea. He had always coveted Andy's boat, which, as we know, was much better than his own had been. It occurred to him that here would be a good opportunity to get it for a trifle.

"Pa," he said, "will you do me a favor?"

"What is it?" asked his father suspiciously.

"You know I haven't got a boat now. Won't you let Mr. Grant pay part of the interest in Andy's boat?"

"What do I want with the boat?" asked the squire impatiently.

"Pa, you can make a great bargain. I hear that it cost seventy-five dollars. You can allow the farmer twenty dollars, and sell it for forty dollars cash."

"I don't know about that."

But the squire's tone was less decided. He liked a bargain, and he knew that there was some logic to what Conrad said.

"Mr. Grant might not feel at liberty to sell his son's boat," he argued.

"Andy would let him. He thinks a good deal of his family."

"I'll think of it, but I intended to propose taking two of his cows."

"That you can do next time. Probably he won't have the interest six months from now."

"I'll see about it."

"There is one other thing -- you would have a better chance to sell the boat for a profit than the cows."

"Well, Conrad, I will think of it, as I said. I am going around to Farmer Grant's this evening, and I will broach the subject."

Later in the day Conrad met Jimmy Morris.

"Have you heard the news, Conrad?" asked Jimmy.

"What is it?"

"Andy Grant is in Arden. He arrived from the city this morning."

"I am glad to hear it."

"Why? Are you and Andy such great friends?"

"It isn't on account of friendship; it's on account of business."

"What business?"

"I can't tell you, but you will very likely hear soon."

Conrad hoped to meet Andy and broach the subject of buying the boat. He decided from his knowledge of the farmer's son that, much as he valued his boat, he would be willing to sacrifice it for the sake of his father. In this thought he paid an unconscious tribute to Andy, for in similar circumstances he would have been incapable of anything so unselfish.

About half-past seven, Andy, looking out of the window, saw the stately and dignified figure of Squire Carter coming up the front path.

"The squire is coming, father," he said. "I want you to look sober, just as if you were unprepared to pay the interest."

Squire Carter had already been informed by Conrad that Andy was in the village. He showed no surprise, therefore, when he saw him.

He had also been down to the river and taken a look at Andy's boat. He could see that it was a very handsome one and doubtless worth as much as Conrad reported.

"So you have come home, Andrew?" he said.

"Yes, Squire Carter."

"You haven't lost your place, have you?"

"No, sir. I have come home on a visit."

"Ahem! You arrived at an unfortunate time for your father. He has had bad luck. Things seem to have gone against him."

"So I heard, sir."

"If you had been at home to help him on the farm, things would have been different, maybe."

"I hope to help him by staying in the city."

"That isn't very likely. I don't approve, for my part, of boys leaving home to work."

"I think I shall succeed in the end, sir."

"Ahem! I have no doubt you think so, but boys like you haven't much judgment. I suppose you know that interest is due on the mortgage for the first six months, and that your father can't meet it."

"I have heard so, Squire Carter."

"As a friend of your father I have a plan to propose that may make things easy for him. I am glad to see you, for a part of my business is with you."

CHAPTER XXIX

THE INTEREST IS PAID

Andy was surprised by the squire's words. He could not conjecture what business Squire Carter could have with him.

"First," said the squire, "may I ask, Mr. Grant, whether you can pay the interest on the mortgage which I hold when it comes due?"

"I have only twenty-five dollars at my command now, Squire Carter. Perhaps something may turn up between now and next Tuesday."

"That is extremely likely," said the squire in a tone of sarcasm.

"Have you anything to propose? Are you willing to wait a month?"

"No, sir. I am not. It will be extreme folly on my part. Do you expect to come into a fortune within thirty days?"

"No, sir."

"So I presume. However, I have a plan to propose. I did intend to say that I would allow you fifty dollars for your two best cows. But even that would not pay the deficit. I believe your son owns a boat."

"I do," said Andy looking up. He began to understand the squire's plan.

"I am willing to allow twenty dollars for it, as my son has taken a fancy to it, and his own boat was destroyed through the malice of a tramp. This, with fifty dollars for your two cows, would pay the interest on all but twenty dollars, which you say you are able to pay in cash."

"Squire Carter, my cows are of a choice breed and are worth fifty dollars each."

"They would not fetch that sum. Indeed, twenty-five dollars each is all that you would have any chance of getting. If you doubt it, you may try to get an offer elsewhere."

"What should I do without the cows? I depend on the butter and milk I obtain from them for a good part of my cash income."

"That is your concern," said the squire, shrugging his shoulders.

"You don't appear to have much consideration for me."

"Business is business, Mr. Grant. You owe me ninety dollars. If you can't pay me in one form, you must in another."

"I would like to say a word, Squire Carter," said Andy. "The boat for which you offer twenty dollars cost Mr. Gale seventy-five."

"I don't believe it."

"I have his word for it."

"Very likely, but it wouldn't be the first case where a man overstated the price of his purchase."

"Mr. Gale would not deceive me in that way."

"Have it as you like. The boat is second-hand now and worth far less than when it was new," persisted the squire.

"There is considerable difference between twenty dollars and seventy-five."

"Well, I might stretch a point and call it twenty-five, as Conrad is desirous of having the boat. In that case there would be five dollars coming to you, which you would doubtless find very handy."

"I think I shall have to decline your offer, Squire Carter."

"And leave your poor father in trouble? I thought better of you."

Squire Carter was surprised to find that both Andy and his father were cool and apparently not suffering anxiety. He had thought they would be sad and would resort to entreaties.

"Does it strike you, Squire Carter, that you are trying to drive a very hard bargain with my father and myself? You offer a very low sum for the cows and for my boat."

"If you can get more anywhere else, you are quite at liberty to do so," said the squire in a tone of indifference.

He felt that father and son were in his power and that he would have his own way in the end.

"I don't think we shall sell at all," said Andy calmly.

"What!" exclaimed the squire. "Not sell at all? Do you think I will allow the interest to remain unpaid?"

"The interest will be paid."

"How? Where will you get the money?"

"I will supply my father with what he needs."

"You talk like a fool!" said the squire sharply. "Do you think I will allow myself to be humbugged by a boy?"

"No, sir, but you can rely upon what I say."

"Have you borrowed the money from Mr. Gale?"

"I have not seen Mr. Gale for several months. He does not know of my father's pecuniary trouble. If he did, I think he would come to his and my assistance. As to the boat, I value it not only on account of its intrinsic worth, but because he gave it to me. Conrad cannot have it."

Squire Carter was much irritated. Besides, he did not believe that Andy would really be able to furnish his father with the help he needed.

"I am not easily deceived, Andrew Grant," he said. "It is useless for me to remain here any longer. I will only say that if the interest is not paid on Tuesday next, your father must take the consequences."

"He is ready to pay it now -- before it is due -- if you will give him a receipt."

"Wh-- what!" exclaimed the squire, in amazement.

"I mean what I say. Father, will you give the squire writing materials and ask him to make out a receipt?"

"Is this -- straight? Are you really able to pay the interest now?"

"Yes, sir. You need have no fear on that score. When my father wrote me about his difficulty I procured the money, and I have it here."

Half incredulous, Squire Carter made out the receipt and a roll of bills was handed to him. He counted them carefully and put them in his wallet.

"The money is correct," he said stiffly. "I am glad you are able to pay it."

"Thanks to Andy here," said his father, with a grateful look at his son.

"All is well so far, but if your son has borrowed the money it will have to be repaid."

"I didn't borrow it, Squire Carter."

"Do you mean to say that you have been able to save it out of your boy's wages?"

"I received it from my employer for special services."

Squire Carter left the house not altogether satisfied. He had received his interest, but he had hoped to profit by the farmer's needs and get what would have been of considerably greater value than the money. In this he had been disappointed.

"But six months hence interest will be due again," he reflected by way of consolation. "This time the Grants were lucky, but they won't be so all the time. Besides, when the mortgage falls due it will take more help than the boy can give to settle it."

When the squire reached home, he found Conrad waiting to see him.

"Well, pa," he said, "am I going to have the boat?"

"No," answered his father shortly.

"Why not? You said you would get it for me."

"They wouldn't sell."

"Then how will they pay the interest?"

"It is paid already."

Conrad opened his eyes wide with amazement.

"Where did the money come from?"

"The boy advanced it to his father."

"You must be joking, pa. Where could Andy get ninety dollars?"

"He only had to supply seventy. As to where it came from, I can't tell. You had better ask him."

"So I will. It's a shame I can't have the boat."

"He wants too much for it."

"How much does he want?"

"I don't know. If he will let you have it for thirty dollars, you can buy it."

"Thank you, pa. It's the same as mine. A boy like Andy can't afford to refuse thirty dollars."

"I don't know. He seems a mighty independent sort of boy."

Conrad lost no time in trying to purchase the boat of Andy, but of course he did so without success.

"I would rather keep it myself," was the reply.

"But you can't use it."

"Not at present, perhaps, but I may be able to some time. Besides, Mr. Gale gave it to me, and I shouldn't be willing to part with it. At any rate, I wouldn't sell for thirty dollars."

"Never mind, Conrad," said his father. "When the next interest is payable, Andrew will probably be glad to accept your offer."

Andy enjoyed the short visit home. He managed to see his friends and promised to look out for positions in the city for two of them. At home his presence was a source of comfort and joy to his mother. It gladdened him to see the bright look on her face, which had been grave and anxious when he arrived.

On Monday morning he set out for New York on an early train, feeling that his visit had been in every way a success. Several boys were at the station to see him off, but among them he did not see Conrad Carter.

CHAPTER XXX

AN UNEXPECTED PROPOSAL

Three months later, when Andy entered the office one morning, he found Mr. Crawford in a thoughtful mood.

"I wish you were older, Andy," he began abruptly.

"Why, sir?"

"Because I have a commission I could then entrust to you."

"Then I am too young for it now?"

"I am afraid so. And yet -- but I will tell you what it is, and see if you consider yourself equal to it. How old are you now?"

"Seventeen, sir."

"I will explain myself. I am intimately acquainted with the men who are engineering the Northern Pacific Railroad, and I have reliable advice that work will at once be resumed on it, and probably the road will be completed in less than a year."

"I suppose this will raise the price of our land in Tacoma?"

"Precisely. Still, I think it will not be advisable to sell for some time to come. My object is rather to buy more land."

"I should think it would be a good idea."

"The time to buy is now, before the public learn of the probable early completion of the railroad. If I could spare the time from my business I would go out there at once."

"I should think it would pay, Mr. Crawford."

"Doubtless it would, but I cannot arrange to leave now. I expect to have some large transactions in real estate during the next two or three months."

"I see the difficulty, sir."

"I will come to the point. Do you think you could go to Tacoma, look carefully over the ground, and secure desirable lots for me?"

"I think I could, sir, under instructions from you."

"That is what I had in mind when I said I wished you were older."

"You could, at any rate, rely upon my faithfully carrying out your instructions."

"I am sure of that, and I also have considerable confidence in your good judgment. At any rate, I will take the risk. What day is today?"

"Thursday."

"Make preparations to start on Monday. Can you do so?"

"Yes, sir."

Andy felt a thrill of delight at the prospect held out to him. He had always felt a strong desire to see the great West but had realized that he should probably have to wait a good many years before his wish was gratified. It had been a dream, but now his dream bade fair to become actuality.

"I will prepare a general letter of instructions and make such suggestions as may occur to me," continued Mr. Crawford. "I will excuse you from office work for the balance of the week, in order that you may make the necessary preparations."

As the Northern Pacific road was not completed, it was decided that Andy should go to San Francisco by the Union Pacific and Central Pacific roads, and take steamer thence to Puget Sound.

"You can stay in San Francisco three days," said Mr. Crawford considerately. "It will give you a chance to rest and see the city."

On Monday Andy started on his long journey. He wrote a brief letter to his mother, as follows:

DEAR MOTHER:

I am going West on some business for Mr. Crawford. I will write you on the way. You are at liberty to tell this to anyone in Arden, but I don't care to have the extent of my journey known. You may think I am young for such a trip, but I have no fears. The business is important, but it is simple, and I hope to carry it through successfully.

In haste, your loving son,

ANDY.

However, Mrs. Grant was not the first one to hear of Andy's trip. It so happened that at the station Andy met Conrad Carter, who had just come into the city for a day.

"How do you happen to be here?" asked Conrad in surprise.

"I am leaving the city."

"I suppose you are discharged and going home," remarked Conrad loftily.

"No, I am going on some business for my employer."

"How far do you go?"

"My first stop will be Chicago."

Conrad was amazed.

"Is this straight?" he asked.

"Yes."

"You are going on business for the firm?"

"Yes."

"Mr. Crawford must be a fool."

"Why?"

"To send an ignorant country boy to Chicago."

Andy smiled.

"Mr. Crawford has succeeded very well in business, and I don't think he is a fool."

"He must be infatuated with you."

"If he is, that is lucky for me."

"How long do you expect to be away?"

"I can't say. I can't tell how long it will take me to transact my business."

"I wish pa would let me go to Chicago," said Conrad enviously. "You are a poor boy, and yet you travel more than I."

"Your time will come, Conrad."

"Has your employer given you much money to travel with?"

"I am to draw on him for what I want."

"Say, won't you write me a letter from Chicago? I wish I had known you were going; I would have asked pa to let me go with you."

Andy was amused at Conrad's change of front. He knew very well that Conrad was no more his friend than before but that his notions were strictly selfish. However, he promised to write to him if he could get time and made the promise in good faith.

"I wish Valentine were going with me," he thought, "but I should not enjoy Conrad's company."

Andy's journey to Chicago was uneventful. About two hours before the train arrived a tall man left his seat on the opposite side of the car and seated himself beside Andy.

"Good morning," he began. "I suppose, like me, you propose to stop in Chicago?"

"For about twenty-four hours," answered Andy.

"And then you go on further?"

"Yes, sir."

"How far?"

"I cannot tell you definitely," answered Andy, who thought it wise to be on his guard.

"Could you oblige me with small bills for a ten? I am owing a dollar to the porter."

Andy took out a large-sized wallet from an inner pocket and opened it. It contained about fifty dollars in bills of different denominations.

"I am afraid I cannot accommodate you," he said, "unless two five-dollar bills will answer your purpose."

"I am afraid it won't help me."

"I am sorry," said Andy politely.

He did not observe the covetous glance of the stranger as he noted the large wallet and its contents. It occurred to him afterward that his companion had not produced the bill he wished changed.

"Oh, well," said the stranger carelessly, "it doesn't matter. I can get the bill changed at the depot. Are you traveling on business?" he inquired.

"Yes, sir."

"So am I. I represent the firm of Arnold & Constable, in New York. Doubtless you have heard of them."

"Oh, yes. They are well known."

"I have been in their employ for five years. Before that I worked for Claflin."

"Indeed!"

"You do not mention the name of your firm."

"No, I am traveling on private business for the head of the firm."

"Ah, yes. I don't wish to be inquisitive. You do right to keep the business to yourself."

"You see, it is not my business."

"Just so! You are young for a business agent."

"That is true, but I am growing older every day."

"Exactly so! Good joke!"

Andy's companion laughed quite heartily, rather to the surprise of his young acquaintance.

"I am very glad to have met you. You see, I am very social and can't stand being alone. By the way, where do you stop in Chicago?"

"At the Sherman House."

"Good hotel! I have stopped there often. Still, there is nothing as homelike as a private house. I have a friend living in the city who keeps a first-class boarding house and only charges transient guests a dollar and a quarter a day. I wish you could be induced to go there with me. At the hotel you will have to pay three or four dollars."

Now, Andy was naturally economical and thought it would be praiseworthy to save money for Mr. Crawford. He inquired the location of the boarding house and imprudently decided to act on his companion's proposal.

CHAPTER XXXI

THE TRAP

Andy left the depot with his new acquaintance, who gave his name as Percival Robinson, and following his lead boarded a horse car, which took them both a distance of three miles to the southern part of the city. As they went on, dwellings became scarce.

"Your friend's house seems quite out of the way," said Andy.

"Yes, but Chicago is a city of distances. It really doesn't make much difference where you stop. Street cars will carry you anywhere."

"Still it would be pleasanter to be centrally located."

"But by going some way out you get cheaper accommodations."

"That is true," thought Andy, "and I have time enough."

At length Robinson signaled to the conductor to stop.

Andy followed him out of the car. They seemed to be in the very outskirts of the city.

Robinson led the way to a rather shabby brick house standing by itself. It was three stories in height.

"This is where my friend lives," he said, walking up the front steps and ringing the front doorbell.

Two minutes later the door was opened by a red-haired man in his shirt sleeves.

"Hello, Tom!" he exclaimed.

"I thought his name was Percival," Andy said to himself.

"My young friend and I will stay overnight with you," said Robinson.

"All right. Come in."

A door on the left was opened, and Andy saw a sanded floor and on one side of the room a bar.

"Go in there a minute," said Robinson, "while I speak to my friend."

Andy went in and picked up a copy of the Clipper from the table -- the only paper in the room.

In five minutes the two returned.

"I'll take your gripsack," said the man in shirt sleeves. "I will show you to your room."

They went up two flights of stairs to a room on the third floor. It was a small apartment about ten feet square, with a double bed in one corner.

"I guess you'll both be comfortable here," said the landlord.

"I think I would rather have a room to myself," said Andy by no means satisfied.

"Sorry we can't accommodate you, for the house is full."

It didn't look so, but then the lodgers might be out.

Andy thought for a moment he would go downstairs and take a car back to the central part of the city, but he was afraid his action would seem strange, and he made no objection.

"I guess we'll get along together," said Robinson in an easy tone.

Andy didn't think so, but he found it awkward to make objections.

"I will take a wash," he said, seeing that the pitcher on the washstand contained water.

"All right!" returned Robinson. "Just make yourself at home. I'll go downstairs. You'll find me there."

Left alone, Andy reproached himself for his too ready yielding to the plans of his companion. He wondered why he had done so.

"Mr. Crawford didn't ask me to be economical," he reflected. "He is willing I should pay ordinary prices at a hotel. I think I have been very foolish. However, I am in for it. It will serve as a lesson to me, which I will remember hereafter."

He looked out the window. There was a lot behind the hotel -- if it was a hotel -- covered with ashes, tin cans, and other litter.

"I am sure," thought Andy, "this isn't the kind of hotel Mr. Crawford wished me to stay at."

When he had washed he went downstairs. As he passed the door of the barroom he saw Mr. Robinson inside, sitting at the table, with a bottle and a glass before him.

"Come in, Grant, and have some whisky," he said.

"Thank you, but I don't care for whisky."

"Perhaps you would prefer beer?"

"I don't care to drink anything, thank you."

"You don't mean to say you're a temperance crank?"

"Yes, I think I am."

"Oh, well, do just as you please. By the way, it is the rule here to pay for board in advance."

"How much is it?"

"A dollar and a quarter, please," said this red-haired man who stood behind the bar.

Andy paid over the money.

"I thought perhaps you would stay more than one day."

"No, I have little time. I shall have to leave tomorrow. I think, Mr. Robinson, I will go out and take a walk."

"All right! Supper will be ready in two hours."

Andy nodded.

He had a great mind to go upstairs and get his gripsack. Then he would be able to go where he pleased. He went out and began to walk about in the neighborhood of the hotel.

It did not seem to be a very pleasant quarter of the city, and it was certainly a good distance from the center.

"I sha'n't learn much about Chicago if I stay here," he thought.

Again he execrated his folly in so weakly yielding to the representations of a man he knew nothing about.

He walked for half an hour and then returned slowly. There didn't seem to be much to look at, and his walk had no interest for him.

Not far from the hotel he met a well-dressed boy and was impelled to speak to him.

"Do you live nearby?" he asked.

"No, but I have an uncle living in that house over there. I came to spend the day with my cousins."

"I am a stranger in this city. I met a man who took me to that brick house. He recommended it as a cheap boarding place. Do you know anything about it?"

"I know that it has a bad reputation."

"Will you tell me what you know about it? You will be doing me a favor."

"The bar does a good business in the evening. I have heard of several cases where men who put up there complained of being robbed."

"Thank you. I am not much surprised to hear it."

"Have you taken a room there?"

"Yes. I am afraid I was foolish."

"I hope you won't be robbed -- that's all."

"I should like to get out, but I am afraid if I come downstairs with my grip they would try to stop my going."

"Where is your room?"

"At the back part of the house, looking out on the lot."

"I'll tell you what you can do," said the other boy after a moment's thought. "Have you paid anything for your room?"

"Yes, but I don't mind that."

"Then drop your grip out of the window. I'll catch it."

"I will."

"Then you can take a car and go down into the city."

"Do you know the way to the Sherman House?"

"Certainly."

"If you will go there with me, I'll make it worth your while."

"All right. I was just about going home, anyway."

"Then I'll go upstairs and get my bag."

Andy went to his room, opened the window, and, looking down, saw his new friend.

"Are you ready?" he asked.

"Yes."

You needn't try to catch it. There's nothing in it that will break."

"Fling her out!"

Andy did so.

"Now come down. You'll find me here."

An hour later supper was served. Percival Robinson and three other men, likewise patrons of the barroom, sat down. The landlord himself was one of the party.

"Where is the kid?" he asked.

"I saw him go out an hour ago," said one of the guests.

"He has probably come back and is in his room," said Robinson. "I will go up and call him."

He went upstairs quickly and entered the room assigned to Andy and himself. It was empty.

"The boy has taken a long walk," he said to himself.

Then he looked about for Andy's grip. It occurred to him that he would have a good opportunity to examine its contents.

He started in surprise and dismay, for the grip was gone.

"He must have given me the slip," he exclaimed.

"Did anyone see the boy go out with his gripsack?" he asked as he returned.

"I saw him go out, but he had nothing in his hand," answered the landlord.

"Well, he's gone, bag and baggage," returned Robinson very much annoyed.

"At any rate, he has paid his bill," said the landlord complacently.

"Bother his hotel bill!" muttered Robinson roughly. "I meant to have a good deal more than that."

"Have you any idea where he has gone?"

"I think he may have gone to the Sherman House. I'll go there after supper and see if I can find him."

CHAPTER XXXII

A CRITICAL MOMENT

Guided by his boy companion, Andy found the Sherman House and registered there. The change was a very satisfactory one, and he enjoyed the comfortable room to which he was assigned.

After a hearty supper he took a seat in the office and watched with interest the crowds that surged in and out of the hotel. Presently he saw a familiar figure entering.

The Sherman House in Chicago in the late 1800s.

It was his late companion, Percival Robinson. The latter was not long in recognizing the boy.

He walked up to the chair on which Andy was seated and addressed him with a look of anger.

"So I have found you, have I?" he said roughly.

Andy knew that this man had no right to interfere with him, and answered coolly, "So it seems."

"Why did you play me such a mean trick, boy?"

"My name is Andrew," said Andy with dignity. "What right have you to speak to me in this manner?"

"I'll tell you presently. You have made a nice return for my kindness."

"I know of no kindness. You got acquainted with me on the train and took me to a house where I didn't care to stop."

"Why didn't you care to stop there?"

"Because I found that it didn't have a good reputation. My employer wouldn't care to have me stay at such a house."

"You are mighty independent for a young boy. I want you to return the wallet of which you relieved me."

Andy was startled at this reckless charge.

"What do you mean?" he demanded hotly. "You know that this is a falsehood."

"We'll see if you will brazen it out. If you don't give me back the wallet, which I have no doubt you have in your pocket at this moment, I will have you arrested."

Andy began to feel nervous. He was a stranger in Chicago. There was no one to identify him or vouch for his honesty. What if this man should carry out his threat and have him arrested?

However, Andy had pluck and didn't intend to surrender at discretion.

This conversation had attracted the attention of two or three guests of the hotel, who were disposed to look with suspicion upon Andy. His accuser appeared like a man of good position, being well dressed and with an air of assurance.

One old gentleman, who was fond of giving advice, said, reprovingly, "My boy, you will find it best to hand the gentleman his wallet. It is sad to see one so young guilty of theft."

"Perhaps the boy is not guilty," suggested another guest.

"I am in the employ of a gentleman in New York," said Andy, "and this man is scheming to rob me."

"You are perfectly shameless!" said Robinson, encouraged by what the old gentleman had said. "I will give you just five minutes to return my wallet, or I will have you arrested."

Andy felt that he was in a tight place, but his wits had not deserted him.

"As you claim the wallet," he said, "perhaps you will tell how much money there is in it."

"I can't tell exactly," replied Robinson. "I spend money liberally, and I have not counted the money lately."

"That is quite reasonable," said the old gentleman. "I don't know how much money there is in my wallet."

"What is there besides money in the wallet?" asked Andy, following up his advantage.

"I think there are a few postage stamps," answered Robinson at a guess.

"You certainly have a good deal of assurance, young man," said the old gentleman in a tone of reproof. "If I were in this gentleman's place I would summon a policeman at once."

"I prefer to give the boy a chance," said Robinson, who had his own reasons for not bringing the matter to the knowledge of the police. "I don't want to get him into trouble. I only want my money back."

"You are more considerate than he deserves," said Andy's critic. "And by the way, here is the hotel detective. Officer, will you come here, please? Here is a case that requires your attention."

The hotel detective, a quiet-looking man, approached.

Robinson was far from thanking the old gentleman for his officiousness. He feared recognition.

"What is the matter?" asked the detective coming up and eying Robinson sharply.

The old gentleman volunteered an explanation.

The detective seemed amused.

"So this man charges the boy with robbing him?" he asked.

"Yes, sir, and we all believe that he has good grounds for doing so."

"I don't believe it," said the gentleman who had already spoken for Andy.

"What have you to say, my boy?" asked the detective, turning to Andy.

"Only that I made the acquaintance of this man on the train. He induced me to go to a small hotel on the outskirts of the city, on the ground that I could board there cheaply. What I saw and heard there excited my suspicions, and I left the place without his knowledge."

"Taking my wallet with you. I incautiously laid it on the bed. When I went up later I found that it and you had disappeared."

"Do you hear that, officer?" asked the old gentleman triumphantly.

"I do," answered the detective. Then, turning to Robinson with a change of tone, he asked, "How did you get so much money, Tom Maitland?"

Robinson turned pale. He saw that he was recognized.

"I will let the matter drop," he said. "I don't want to get the boy into trouble."

He turned toward the door, but the detective was too quick for him.

"You will have to go with me," he said. "You have been trying a bold confidence game. I shall have to lock you up."

"Gentlemen," said Robinson turning pale, "will you permit this outrage?"

"It is an outrage!" said the old gentleman hotly.

"My friend," inquired the detective, "do you know this man?"

"No, but -- "

"Then let me introduce him as Tom Maitland, one of the cleverest confidence men in Chicago."

He produced a pair of handcuffs, which he deftly slipped over the wrists of Percival Robinson, and led him out of the hotel.

Andy was satisfactorily vindicated and, it must be admitted, enjoyed the discomfiture of the old gentleman, who slunk away in confusion.

When Andy set out on his journey he intended to go to Tacoma by way of San Francisco but found, as he proceeded, that he could go by the Northern Pacific as far as it was built, and proceed the rest of the way by stage and over Puget Sound. This seemed to him to afford greater variety, and he adopted the plan.

Some hundreds of miles east of his destination he took the stage. It was rather a toilsome mode of traveling, but he obtained a good idea of the country through which he was passing.

At that time stage robberies were frequent, nor have they wholly ceased now. Among the stage robbers who were most dreaded was a certain Dick Hawley, who had acquired a great reputation for daring and was known to have been engaged in nearly twenty stage robberies.

**"The Deadwood Stagecoach" traveling through
the American west in 1889.**

As they approached that part of the route in which he operated, there was a great anxiety manifested by the passengers and especially by a thin, cadaverous-looking man from Ohio.

"Do you think we shall meet Dick Hawley today, driver?" he asked.

"I can't say, sir. I hope not."

"How often have you met him?"

"Three times."

"Did he rob the stage every time?"

"Yes."

"Were there many passengers on board?" asked Andy.

"Nearly ten every time."

"And they allowed one man to rob them?"

"Wait till you meet him," said the driver, shrugging his shoulders.

"If he stops the stage I shall die of fright," said the cadaverous-looking man. "I know I shall."

"Have you a good deal of money with you?" asked a fellow passenger.

"I have ninety-seven dollars and a half," answered the other soberly.

"Better lose that than die! If you give it up, there won't be any danger of bodily injury."

The cadaverous-looking man groaned but did not reply.

Gradually they ascended, for they were among the mountains, till they reached a narrow ledge or shelf scarcely wider than the stage. On one side there was a sheer descent of hundreds of feet and great caution was requisite.

Just at the highest point a horseman appeared around a curve and stationed himself directly in front of the stage with a revolver pointed at the driver.

"Stop and give up your money, or I fire!" he exclaimed.

It was the dreaded highwayman, Dick Hawley.

CHAPTER XXXIII

A SUDDEN TRAGEDY

The driver pulled up short. The passengers realized that something had happened, and the nervous man put his head out of the window.

Instantly a change came over his face.

"We are all dead men!" he groaned. "It is the highwayman!"

Andy felt startled in spite of his pluck, and so did the other passengers.

"I would jump out and confront the scoundrel," said a determined-looking man, "but there is no room. We are on the verge of a precipice."

"What will happen?" exclaimed the cadaverous-looking man in an agony of terror.

"I suppose we shall be robbed. That will be better than tumbling over the precipice."

"Oh, why did I ever leave home?"

"I don't know. Ask me something easier," said the resolute man in disgust. "Such a man as you ought never to stir from his own fireside."

"Stop the coach and pass over your watches and pocketbooks!" cried Dick Hawley in a commanding tone.

By way of exciting alarm and enforcing his order he fired one charge of his revolver. The consequences he did not anticipate.

The terrified stage horses, alarmed by the report, got beyond control of the driver and dashed forward impetuously. The highwayman had hardly time to realize his danger when his horse was overthrown and pushed over the precipice along with its rider, while the stage dashed on. The last that the passengers saw of Dick Hawley was a panic-stricken face looking upward as he fell rapidly down toward the rocks at the bottom.

"He's gone! We are saved!" exclaimed the cadaverous-looking man joyfully.

"That is, if the coach doesn't tumble after him."

But the coach was saved. Had the horses swerved in their course all would have been killed. As it was, the dangerous place was safely crossed and the stage emerged upon a broad plateau.

The driver stopped the horses and, dismounting from the box, came around to the coach door.

"I congratulate you, gentlemen," he said. "We had a close shave, but we are out of danger. Dick Hawley will rob no more stages."

"Driver, you are a brave man -- you have saved us," said one of the passengers.

"It was not I; it was the horses."

"Then you did not start them up?"

"No. I should not have dared to do it. They were frightened by the revolver and took the matter into their own hands."

"Dick Hawley was foolhardy. Had he ever stopped a stage at this point before?"

"Yes, he did so last year."

"And succeeded?"

"Yes. He made a big haul. This time he has met his deserts."

There were no further incidents that deserve recording in Andy's journey. It is needless to say that he enjoyed it. The scenes through which he passed were new and strange to him. It was a country he had never expected to see, and for this reason, perhaps, he enjoyed it all the more.

At last he reached Tacoma. It was irregularly built on a hillside. There were no buildings of any pretensions. All its importance was to come.

He put up at the Tacoma House, a hotel of moderate size, and after dinner he went out to see the town. He sought out the plot of lots owned jointly by Mr. Crawford and himself, and found that they were located not far from the center of the business portion of the town.

It took no sagacity to foresee that the land would rise in value rapidly, especially after the Northern Pacific Railroad was completed.

In the afternoon, feeling tired, he sat in his room and read a book he had picked up at a periodical store -- a book treating of the great Northwest. The partitions were thin and noises in the adjoining room were easily audible.

His attention was drawn to a sound of coughing and a groan indicating pain. It was evident that the next apartment was occupied by a sick man.

Andy's sympathies were excited. It seemed to be a forlorn position to be sick and without attention in this remote quarter. After a moment's hesitation he left his own room and knocked at the other door.

"Come in!" was the reply in a hollow voice.

Andy opened the door and entered.

On the bed lay a man, advanced in years, with hollow cheeks and every appearance of serious illness.

"I am afraid you are very sick," said Andy gently.

"Yes. I have an attack of influenza. I am afraid I will have to pass in my checks."

"Oh, it isn't as bad as that," said Andy in a reassuring tone. "Have you no one to take care of you?"

"No. Everybody here is occupied with schemes for money-making. I can't get anyone to look after me for love or money."

"Then you have no near friend or relative in Tacoma?"

"No; nor, I may say, anywhere else. I have a niece, however, in Syracuse. She is at school. She is the only tie, the only one on whom I have any claim."

"If you need money -- " began Andy feeling a little delicate about offering pecuniary assistance.

"No, I have no need of that kind. I suppose I look poor, for I never cared about my personal appearance, but I am one of the largest owners of real estate in Tacoma, besides having some thousands of dollars in a San Francisco bank. But what good will it all do me? Here I am, sick, and perhaps near death."

"I will do what I can for you," said Andy. "I am myself a visitor in Tacoma. I came on business for a New York gentleman. I am authorized to buy lots in Tacoma. When you are better, I will make you an offer for your land, if you care to sell."

"Help me to get well, and you shall have it on your own terms."

"You will need someone besides myself. Do you authorize me to hire an attendant?"

"Yes, I shall be glad to have you do so. I begin to hope for recovery, through your assistance. I had given myself up for lost."

"Then I will go out and see what I can do. Do you authorize me to pay liberally for the service of a nurse?"

"Pay anything -- fifty dollars a week, if necessary. I can afford it."

"I will go out at once. I will see if I can buy some oranges."

Andy left the hotel and walked toward the steamboat wharf. It was deserted, except by two persons.

A young man of thirty, bronzed by exposure to the weather and who looked like a farmer, stood beside a plain, cheap trunk, on which sat a woman somewhat younger, who had a weary and anxious look.

The young man -- her husband, doubtless -- seemed troubled.

"Good afternoon," said Andy pleasantly. "Are you in any trouble? Is there anything I can do for you?"

"Well, my boy, I'm in a tight place. I came here from Iowa, with my wife, expecting to meet a cousin who had promised to get me employment. I find he has left Tacoma. So here I am, with less than five dollars in my pocket and no prospect of work. I'm not a coward, but I don't mind saying I'm afraid to think of what will become of us."

An idea came to Andy.

Here was a chance to secure a nurse.

"Is your wife used to sickness?" he asked. "Could she take care of a sick man?"

The woman brightened up.

"I took care of my father for a year," she answered. "I'm a middlin' good nurse."

"She's the best nurse I know of," put in her husband.

"All right! Then I can find you employment. An acquaintance of mine, an old man - -as old, probably, as your father -- is sick with grip at the Tacoma House. He will pay you liberally. Can you come with me at once?"

"Yes, and be glad to."

"Come, then. You will be paid twenty-five dollars a week."

"Why that's a fortune!" said the woman amazed.

"Come with me at once, and your husband can follow at his leisure."

"Maria, that's what I call a streak of good luck," said her husband overjoyed. "Go along with this young man, and I'll get a cheap room somewhere in town. I'll take the trunk along with me."

He shouldered the small trunk, and his wife went off with Andy.

In a few minutes she was installed in the sick chamber and soon showed that she understood her business. A doctor was sent for, and Seth Johnson, for this was the sick man's name, was soon made comfortable.

He ratified Andy's bargain and paid, besides, for Mrs. Graham's board at the hotel. He did not gain rapidly, for his strength was at a low ebb, but he improved steadily.

Maria takes good care of Seth Johnson while he is ill.

The husband found employment in a couple of days, and their temporary despondency gave place to hope and courage.

"You've done better for me than my cousin would have done, Andy," said Graham a few days later. "You've set me on my feet, and I'm not afraid now but I'll get along."

CHAPTER XXXIV

SETH JOHNSON'S GIFT

It was four weeks before Seth Johnson became convalescent. His system was run down, and he was in a very critical state when found by Andy. Careful nursing saved him.

When able to get out, he accompanied Andy to show him his lots. The plot was about as large as Mr. Crawford's but was a little further from the center of the town. It would make about twenty-five lots of the average size.

"How much will you take for the entire plot?" asked Andy.

"I don't want to sell the whole," said Johnson.

"I thought you meant to leave Tacoma for good?"

"So I do, but I propose to give one-fifth of the land to a friend."

"Then let me know how much you will take for the remaining four-fifths."

"Will five thousand dollars be too much?"

"I will buy it at that figure," said Andy promptly.

"You don't ask me to whom I intend to give the fifth which I reserve?"

"It is probably no one whom I know."

"On the contrary, it is one whom you know well -- it is yourself."

Andy looked amazed.

"But how have I deserved such a gift?" he asked.

"You have saved my life. If you had not found and befriended me, I should not have been living at this moment. 'All that a man hath will he give in exchange for his life,' the Bible says. I don't give all, but I give merely one-fifth of my land. I have ten thousand dollars, besides, in San Francisco."

"I am deeply grateful to you, Mr. Johnson. I am a poor boy, and this unexpected gift will help me to carry out some plans for the benefit of my father, who is in an embarrassed condition."

"I advise you not to sell the land till you can sell at an advanced price."

"I shall not do so. When the Northern Pacific is completed I am sure lots will be much higher."

"To be sure. You are young and can wait. I am old, and I have no particular desire to make money. I have enough to see me through."

When Andy started for New York he had the company of Seth Johnson. It was agreed that the final arrangements for the transfer of the lots should take place in Mr. Crawford's office.

They reached the city without adventure, and Andy, with his new friend, reported at his employer's.

"I hope you are satisfied with what I have done, Mr. Crawford," said Andy.

"Thoroughly so. You have made a good purchase. I shall pay you five hundred dollars as an acknowledgment of the service you have rendered me."

"But, Mr. Crawford, Mr. Johnson has already given me five lots."

"True, but this is his gift, not mine. You must not be afraid of becoming too rich. You will need all your money."

"Yes, sir, but not for myself. I can now relieve my father's anxiety."

"Do you intend to tell him the amount of your good fortune?"

"I will only tell him of your gift."

On the basis of the sum which Mr. Crawford paid for the other four-fifths, Andy's share of Mr. Johnson's land amounted to twelve hundred and fifty dollars. But when, three months later, active operations for the extension and completion of the railroad commenced, it could easily have been sold for double.

But Andy was too sagacious to sell. In a year his father's mortgage would be payable, and he wanted to be prepared for that.

Meanwhile Andy devoted himself with energy to mastering the details of the real estate business. Perhaps because he now himself owned real estate, he became very much interested in it. He was not able often to visit Arden, but he never let a week pass without writing a letter home.

It was usually addressed to his mother, as his father was more accustomed to guiding the plow than the pen. He also heard occasionally from his friends. No letters were more welcome than those of Valentine Burns. About three months before the mortgage became due he received the following from Valentine:

DEAR ANDY:

I wish I could see you more often, but I know you are busy and getting on. That is a great satisfaction to me. Your last letter informing me that you had been raised to fifteen dollars a week gave me much pleasure. I wanted to tell Conrad, only you didn't wish to have me. He is getting prouder and more disagreeable every day. He really seems to have a great spite against you, though I cannot understand why.

I met him the other day, and he inquired after you. 'He hasn't been to Arden lately,' he said.

'No,' I answered, 'he is too busy.'

'Probably he can't afford the railway fare,' said Conrad.

'I think he is getting good pay,' I said.

'I know better. He isn't getting over six dollars at most,' said Conrad.

'Did he tell you so?' I asked.

'No, but I heard on good authority,' he replied.

'I wish I were getting that,' I said.

'You wouldn't want to live on it,' he rejoined.

'Well, perhaps not,' I admitted.

'He won't long have a home to come back to,' said Conrad after a pause.

'Why not?' I inquired.

'My father holds a mortgage on his father's farm, and it will fall due in three months,' he answered.

'Surely he won't foreclose?'

'Surely he will,' returned Conrad. 'Old Grant will have to leave the farm and go to the poorhouse or, at any rate, to some small place like the Sam Martin house. It contains four rooms and is good enough for a bankrupt.'

This made me uneasy. I hope, Andy, you will find some friend who will be able and willing to advance money to pay the mortgage when it falls due. I hear Squire Carter is working with a city man to buy the place. He evidently feels sure that it will come into his possession.

When Andy read this portion of the letter he smiled.

"I suspect Conrad and his father will be disappointed," he said to himself. "The city man will have to look elsewhere for an investment."

One day Andy had a pleasant surprise. Just in front of him on Broadway he saw a figure that looked familiar.

The tall, bent form, and long white hair he recognized at once as belonging to Dr. Crabb, the principal of Penhurst Academy.

He pressed forward.

"Dr. Crabb!" he exclaimed. "It is long since we have met. I hope you are well."

Dr. Crabb surveyed him with a puzzled look. Andy had grown so much that he could not place him.

"I suppose you are one of my old pupils," he said, "but I shall have to ask your name."

"Don't you remember Andy Grant?"

"Bless my soul! Is it possible? Why, you have grown much taller and larger."

"Yes, sir. I don't want to stand still."

"And what are you doing now?"

"I am in business in this city."

"That is well, but it is a great pity you could not have remained at school."

"I thought so myself at the time I left, but I'm quite reconciled to the change now."

"Doubtless you are doing your duty, wherever you are. In what business are you engaged?"

"I am in a real estate office."

"I hope you are making fine wages?"

"I receive fifteen dollars a week."

"Bless my soul! Why, that is all I pay my head assistant. You must be doing a great job. And how is your father?"

"He is pretty well, sir, but his loss of property has worn upon him."

"Naturally. Did I not understand that he had to mortgage his farm."

"Yes, sir."

"I hope there is no danger of foreclosure?"

"There might be, sir, but when the danger comes I shall be able to help him."

"I am not much of a capitalist, Andy. I understand Latin and Greek better than I do investments, but if a loan of a few hundred dollars will help him I shall be willing to let him have it."

"Thank you very much, Dr. Crabb, but my employer, Mr. Crawford, will give me all the help I need."

"I am truly pleased to hear it. I wish you were able to return to the academy. You were our primus, and I did not like to spare you. You might in time have succeeded me."

"I hope it will be a long time before you require a successor, doctor. I shall confine my ambitions to succeeding in my business."

CHAPTER XXXV

THE RETURN OF AN OLD FRIEND

One afternoon Andy was busy writing in the office when he heard himself called by name and, looking up, saw Walter Gale, who had just entered.

"Mr. Gale!" he exclaimed joyfully, rising and grasping the hands of his friend.

"So you know me? Upon my word, you have grown so that I find it difficult to recognize you."

"Yes, I believe I have grown taller."

"And more grown up. I need not ask if you are well. Your appearance answers that question."

"I was never better."

"And you enjoy your work?"

"Immensely. But when did you reach the city?"

"This morning. As you see, I have lost no time in looking you up."

"Shall you stay here now?"

"Yes," answered Gale gravely. "My poor uncle is dead. His sickness was a painful one, and he is better off."

"I am glad you are to be in the city. I hope to see you often."

"You will, if I can have my way. I have hired a handsome and roomy flat on Madison Avenue, and I expect you to come and live with me."

"I shall be delighted to do so if you will let me pay my share of the expenses."

"You will pay me with your company. I will receive no other pay. My uncle has left me all his property -- at least a hundred thousand dollars -- and I was rich before."

"I will certainly accept your offer since I am sure you will like to have me."

"You were teaching a boy, I believe?"

"Yes, but he is so well advanced now that he does not need my assistance. I am free to accept your kind offer."

"Call upon me this evening and arrange to move tomorrow. I am very lonely and want young and cheerful company."

When Andy called upon his friend in the evening he found him sumptuously lodged. The next evening he moved in.

"What news from Arden, Andy?" asked Mr. Gale.

"Nothing much, except that Squire Carter is expecting to foreclose the mortgage on father's farm next week."

"Is that so? We must not permit that."

"No. I have a thousand dollars in the bank, and I shall ask Mr. Crawford tomorrow if he will advance me two thousand on some lots I own in Tacoma."

"That will not be necessary. I will myself advance the full amount, and you can pay me whenever you sell your lots."

"That is very kind, Mr. Gale and relieves me very much."

"Don't overestimate the kindness. I have more money than I know what to do with."

"There are others in the same position who would not help me."

"I am your friend. That makes the difference. When you go to Arden I will go, too. It will be pleasant for me to see the place where I passed so enjoyable a summer and made so good a friend."

"I shall be delighted to have your company, Mr. Gale."

Two evenings later, as Andy was walking up Broadway toward his new home, he saw a familiar figure in front of him -- the figure of a boy about his own age. Evidently the boy had been drinking and could not walk straight.

Once, as he turned half around, Andy, with a start, recognized John Crandall who had treated him so meanly at Mr. Flint's. He had no reason to like him, but his compassion was aroused.

"John," said Andy linking his arm in his, "how do you happen to be in this condition?"

"Who are you?" hiccoughed John.

"I am Andy Grant. Don't you know me?"

"Yes, you used to be at Mr. Flint's. Where are you taking me?" he asked suspiciously.

"To my room. I will take care of you tonight. What are you doing now?"

"I was in a place on Wall Street, but I got bounced yesterday. I took the money they paid me and got drunk."

"That was foolish. Where is your uncle?"

"He has gone to Chicago. I'm awful unlucky, Andy."

"If you will turn over a new leaf and stop drinking, I'll see if I can't get you another place."

"Will you?" asked John hopefully. "Don't you hate me?"

"No."

172

"I should think you would. I got you out of Flint's."

"You did me a service without intending it."

"You're a good fellow," hiccoughed John. "I'm sorry I treated you so mean."

"I'm not, since it led to my securing my present place. But we must turn down here."

"Where do you live?"

"On Madison Avenue."

"Madison Avenue? You must be a success."

Andy smiled.

"If you work hard you may become successful, too."

When they entered the flat, John stared about him in amazement.

"How can you afford to live in such a fine place?" he said.

"Because a friend bears the greater part of the expense. We have a spare room, and I will let you occupy it. In the morning I will wake you up for breakfast."

John Crandall was soon fast asleep. A few minutes later Mr. Gale came in.

"We have a visitor tonight," said Andy.

"A friend of yours?"

"He may become so, but thus far he has been anything but that."

Andy told the story of John's attempt to injure him.

"And yet you befriend him?"

"Yes. Wouldn't you?"

Walter Gale smiled.

"Tell me your reasons," he said.

"I have no grudge against him. Besides, if we only benefit those whom we like, there isn't much credit in that."

"Exactly. There isn't much credit in my doing you favors."

"Don't think I am ungrateful, Mr. Gale. I appreciate all you have done for me."

"I understand you, Andy, and I like you better for what you have done. What further plans have you?"

"I should like to get John a place and give him a chance to redeem himself. He needs a friend badly."

"He shall have one. We will both help him."

When John Crandall awoke the next morning he was himself again. The effects of his intoxication had passed off, and he seemed ashamed of the predicament in which Andy had found him.

"Have you any home, John?" asked Andy.

"No. That is, I have a room, but I spent all the money that was coming to me, and they won't let me stay. I don't know what I shall do," he said despondently.

"If Mr. Gale and I will find you a new place, will you try to keep it?"

"Yes, I will."

"Then we will stand by you. You can stay here till I come from the office this afternoon, and I will find you a boarding place."

"You are a good fellow, Andy. You are my very best friend."

"I will try to be."

"And I will try to deserve your kindness."

Before the week was out John had a new place on Pearl Street and was an inmate of the boarding house in Clinton Place where Andy stayed when he first came to the city.

He really turned over a new leaf and became a favorite and trusted employee in the Pearl Street store. Andy had saved him.

CHAPTER XXXVI

SAD FOREBODINGS

The day which had been so eagerly awaited by Squire Carter dawned at last. The mortgage on Sterling Grant's farm was due, and he intended to foreclose. There was a gentleman from the city who had taken a fancy to the farm and had offered him eight thousand dollars for it. The squire hoped to obtain it by foreclosure at less than five thousand. This would be taking advantage of the farmer, but, as the squire said to himself complacently, "Business is business!" These words are used as an excuse for a great many mean acts.

At supper time the evening before Sterling Grant looked sad and troubled.

"Dear," he said to Mrs. Grant, "I am afraid we shall have to bid goodbye to the old farm tomorrow."

"Do you really think the squire will foreclose, Sterling?"

"I know he will. I called on him today and begged and pleaded with him to extend the mortgage another year, but it was all in vain."

"I don't see how people can be so hard-hearted," said Mrs. Grant indignantly.

"It's the squire's nature. He says that business is business."

"I thought perhaps Andy might do something. He has five hundred dollars and maybe a little more."

"It would do no good, dear. I hinted that I might be able to pay a part of the mortgage, but the squire wouldn't hear of it. He said the whole or none."

"I am sure Andy would help us if he could."

"I know that, but the mortgage is for three thousand dollars. It is quite beyond his ability to lift."

"I am afraid you are right, Sterling," said his wife with a sigh. "I thought perhaps Andy would be here by this time."

"It would do no good to come unless he brought the money with him."

"He may come yet by the seven o'clock train."

"We had better not count on that, or we shall only be the more disappointed."

"What shall you do, Sterling, if the squire takes the farm?"

"There will be some money left, but I am afraid not much."

"Isn't the place worth six thousand dollars?"

"Yes but it won't fetch that at a forced sale. The squire told me this afternoon that it wasn't worth more than fifteen hundred dollars over and above the face of the mortgage."

"It would be wicked to sell for that."

"We must be content with what we can get."

After supper the farmer took his hat and walked slowly and soberly about the farm. He felt that it was his farewell. Till now it had been his. Tomorrow it would pass from his possession.

"It is hard," he sighed, "but it can't be helped. At any rate, we won't starve."

There was a small house, with half an acre of land attached on the outskirts of the village, which he could get at a moderate rental. He had inquired about it and had made up his mind to secure it.

"But it is humble," objected his wife.

"We must not be proud, dear," he said. We can make it look homelike with our furniture in it."

"But what will you do for an income, Sterling?"

"I can work out by the day. Perhaps the man who buys our farm -- I hear the squire has got a purchaser for it -- will employ me."

"To work out by the day at your age, Sterling!" said his wife indignantly.

"It will be hard, but if it is necessary I can do it."

"But I want to help, Sterling. I can get sewing to do."

"No, no. I won't consent to that."

"Then I won't consent to your working by the day."

"Well, we won't discuss it tonight. We will let the future take care of itself."

Just then the noise of wheels was heard, and a buggy stopped at the door.

"I do believe it's Andy!" exclaimed Mrs. Grant joyfully.

It was Andy. A minute later, he was in the house.

"I am late," he said. "I missed the regular train and had to get off at Stacy, six miles away, but I got a man from the stable to bring me over."

"I am glad to see you, Andy," said his mother.

"And so am I," added Sterling Grant, "though it is a sad time."

"Why a sad time, father?"

"The squire will foreclose tomorrow."

"No, he won't foreclose, father. I will stop it."

"But how can you prevent it, my son?"

176

"By paying the three thousand dollars, father."

"Have you got the money?" asked his father incredulously.

"Yes."

"But how -- ?"

"Don't ask me any questions, father. Be satisfied with the knowledge that I have got it."

"Heaven be praised!" said the farmer fervently.

"I don't think Squire Carter will say that."

CHAPTER XXXVII

CONCLUSION

A little before twelve o'clock on the following day, Squire Carter rang the bell at the farmhouse door. He was dressed with scrupulous neatness, and there was a smile of triumphant anticipation on his face.

Andy answered the bell.

"Walk in, squire," he said.

"Ha! So you are home, Andy?"

"Yes, sir."

"Ahem! Your father has been unfortunate."

"Then you intend to foreclose?"

"Yes. I need the money and must have it."

"Isn't that rather hard on an old neighbor?"

"You are a boy, Andy, and don't understand. Business is business."

"Well, come in."

Mr. and Mrs. Grant were sitting by the fireplace. They looked calm, not sorrowful, as the squire anticipated.

"Ahem! My friends, I am sorry for you!" said the squire in a perfunctory way. "Life is full of disappointments, as we read in the Scriptures."

"What do you propose to do with the farm, squire?" asked the farmer calmly.

"I may sell it, if I can find a purchaser. I haven't thought much about it."

"That is right, squire. It isn't well to count your chickens before they are hatched."

It was Andy who spoke.

"Andrew, you are very flippant," said the squire displeased. "I apprehend that there is very little doubt as to my having the farm to sell."

"What do you suppose is going to become of my father?"

"That is not for me to say. If I run the farm I may hire him to work on it."

"He has made up his mind to work on it."

"With or without my permission?" said the squire with a sneer.

"Exactly so."

"I don't understand you," said the squire with dignified displeasure.

"I presume not, but you will understand better when I say that he stands prepared to pay off the mortgage, and the farm will remain his."

"Impossible!" exclaimed the squire, turning pale.

"Quite possible, sir. Have you the mortgage with you?"

"Yes."

"Here is a release which you will please sign. Father, you had better pay the squire at once."

Mr. Grant took out a big wallet and counted out thirty one-hundred-dollar bills.

"I believe that is correct, squire," he said.

"No, it isn't. You haven't paid the interest," snarled the squire.

"Here is another hundred dollars -- that will cover it."

Ten minutes later Squire Carter left the farmhouse with a heavy frown upon his face. He was bitterly disappointed, and the money did not console him.

This was not the last of his disappointments. His brother's widow in New York sued him for an accounting of his father's estate, and he was obliged, not long afterward, to pay her five thousand dollars. This put the widow and her son in a comfortable position but seriously embarrassed the squire, who had lost money by ill-advised speculation.

Two years later he had to sell his fine place and take a much humbler one half a mile from the village. Conrad was obliged to seek a place and is bitterly humiliated because he receives but four dollars a week, while the boy he used to look down upon is prosperous and successful.

Andy has sold out his property in Tacoma to such advantage that he counts himself worth twenty thousand dollars. He continues to live in handsome style with his friend, Walter Gale, and is to be taken into partnership in the real estate office by Mr. Crawford when he attains the age of twenty-one.

Of the less important characters in our story it may be said that Byron Warren has had a story published in the nickel library and is very proud of this measure of success. He continues to write poems for the Century and other prominent magazines. They always come back to him "respectfully declined," but he cherishes the hope that some day he will receive a more favorable answer.

Valentine Burns holds a place in Mr. Crawford's office and is doing an excellent job. Simon Rich, formerly head clerk for Mr. Flint, has proved a defaulter and is a fugitive in Canada. Sam Perkins still dazzles the world with his showy neckties, but thus far has only risen to ten dollars a week.

Mr. Grant and his wife are happy in Andy's success, and there is no danger of the farm passing from their possession. Quite unexpectedly the farmer has received a check from Nathan Lawrence, the defaulting cashier of the Benton bank, for a thousand dollars, with assurance that in time the entire three thousand dollars will be paid up.

"After all father," writes Andy, "it was lucky for me that I had to leave school. It was the beginning of my present prosperity."

THE END

~ ~ ~

TEACHERS GUIDE QUESTIONS FOR ANDY GRANT'S PLUCK

1. Describe Andy Grant's first encounter with Conrad Carter in Chapter III. Where does the encounter take place, and what does each boy say? How are their temperaments different or similar?

2. In Chapter IV, John Larkin tells Conrad Carter "That don't make you any the better fellow." What does John mean when he says this? How are Valentine or Andy "better fellows" than Conrad?

3. How does Andy react to his first interaction with the tramp on his way to Brenton? How does Andy react during his trip back to Arden when the tramp stops him? What does Andy do to ameliorate the difficult situation?

4. In Chapter IX, Conrad returns home after seeing Andy's new boat for the first time and explains to his father that Andy "is always doing something to annoy me." Does Andy do things to intentionally annoy Conrad? How and why does Conrad come about this conclusion?

5. During his first day in the city, Andy makes two assumptions: first about a man he encounters on the street who inquires for 25¢; second about the type of sickly man Mr. Warren must be. Are Andy's assumptions correct? What does he learn about these two individuals after subsequent encounters with them?

6. What does Andy do and say immediately after Simon Rich's accusations about the gold watch? What does Andy do in the following days?

7. How does Andy become successful in the real estate business? What does he do that directly leads to his success?

8. In Chapter XXVI, Andy learns "a great lesson that some never learn." What is this lesson? How does he learn it? Do you agree that this lesson is important or great? If so, why?

9. What does Andy do when he sees John Crandall in Chapter XXXV? What are Andy's reasons for befriending John? How does Mr. Gale interpret Andy's actions?

TEACHERS GUIDE ANSWERS FOR ANDY GRANT'S PLUCK

1.   Conrad approaches Andy during his walk home. Conrad poses several questions about leaving the Academy and reveals that he thinks Andy's father foolish for sending Andy to the academy in the first place because, "'If the Arden grammar school is good enough for me it is good enough for you.'" He then accuses Andy, a poor farm boy, of being foolish for wanting to go to the academy at all, and Conrad reminds Andy that his father has taken a loan from the Squire, Conrad's father.

      This first encounter paints Conrad as pompous, snobbish and highly concerned with money. Conrad becomes flustered easily and is clearly rude to Andy because of his family's inferior financial position. Though Conrad continues to talk down to Andy, Andy remains calm and offers short, brief answers to his questions. Andy states his opinions independently, and even sarcastically comments that Conrad's "'age and experience make your opinion of value.'"

2.   John Larkin means that though Conrad's father is wealthy, Conrad is certainly not a more respectable or well-liked fellow for it. Valentine or Andy are "better fellows" than Conrad because they are not arrogant and don't show "selfishness on all occasions" as Conrad does.

3.   Andy follows his instinct and declines to offer the tramp a ride as Andy suspects the tramp to have been drinking. On his return home, Andy is nervous but resolute: he is determined not to have any of Mr. Gale's money stolen, and he remains cool and self-possessed. By standing his ground, waiting for help and listening attentively, Andy stalls the tramp while another carriage approaches and helps Andy get out of the difficult situation.

4.   Andy does not do anything to intentionally annoy Conrad, but Conrad comes to this conclusion because he is jealous of Andy's boat, Andy's skill at rowing and even Andy's friendship with Mr. Gale. He is annoyed that though Andy's family does not have as much financial wealth at Conrad's family, Andy is succeeding in school, personal relationships and life.

5.   Andy is incorrect in both assumptions. He too readily trusts the man who inquires for 25¢, later finding out that the story the man tells is a lie. Andy then learns that though he judged Mr. Warren as a sickly, strange man, Andy spends more time with Mr. Warren, gets to know him and realizes that he is a good person.

6.   Andy does not understand where the ticket for the watch came from, and he insists he is innocent. He asks Mr. Rich to accompany him to the pawn shop in order to prove his innocence, but Mr. Rich declines the invitation.

In the next few days, Andy visits the detective shop and receives a description of the young man who actually pawned the watch. In the meantime, he finds another job but clears his name with Mr. Flint, his former employer.

7.   Andy becomes successful in the real estate business by reading and learning as much as he can about real estate. He is willing to take opportunities as they come, including showing and selling a house in the country and acting on a conversation he overhears regarding property in Arizona.

8.   Andy learned that "there is nothing so satisfactory as helping others," or it is far better to give to and help others than anything else. He learns this when he helps Mrs. Carter and her family by providing them with money and securing a job for Mrs. Carter so that she may provide for her family in the future.

9.   When Andy sees John Crandall, Andy helps him, gives him a place to stay and puts him on the right track. Andy befriends John because he holds no grudge against John and because he explains that, "if we only benefit those whom we like, there isn't much credit in that." Mr. Gale thinks of how he befriended Andy whom he did like, and Andy explains that he is grateful to Mr. Gale for it. Mr. Gale likes Andy that much more for his attempt to befriend even his foes.

COMMENTARY FOR ANDY GRANT'S PLUCK

Building The American Hero

By Mark Irwin

About a hundred years after Alger's first triumph in boys' fiction, Ragged Dick (1868) appeared as a twelve-part serial in Student and Schoolmate, my ten-year-old self was pre-occupied with a number of comic book heroes, and almost all of them can be connected in one way or another to Andy Grant. Then as now, most boys I know prefer a hero with a utility belt over a hero with inexplicable superpowers: a Batman over a Superman, an Ironman over a Thor. It's not that they object to extraordinary abilities, but what makes for genuinely exciting reading is the possibility that with a little work and the right combination of events, like their heroes, they too can achieve great things.

And so enter Andy Grant's Pluck (1902), published three years after Horatio Alger, Jr.'s death. As the title suggests, Andy Grant's Pluck might be considered a coda or postscript to the Luck and Pluck series of eight novels which began in 1869 with Luck and Pluck and continued through Herbert Carter's Legacy in 1875. Each of these novels rings variations on the hero leaving home to seek his fortune and, by living honestly and studying hard at whatever task lies before him—with "luck and pluck," in other words, managing to return home in time to pay off the family's mortgage and save the homestead from the local villainous squire.

The late Alger novels were sometimes criticized in their day for their violence—hard to believe today, I know. But when you compare this novel to Mark the Match-Boy or other early novels, you can see the difference. Tastes in America had changed over the thirty or so years Alger was actively publishing, Andy finds his opportunities lie in traveling far from his village home and the city where he is seeking his fortune to the American west, with arsonists, tramps and even an outlaw holding up a stagecoach along the way. I like to think that as America's consciousness of itself as a nation was growing, so, too Alger wanted the boys who were his readers to see beyond the urban boundaries of his earlier novels.

Despite the larger canvas, Alger never loses sight of the essential principles grounding his work. You don't have to think about it very long before you see in the author's purpose an implied understanding that the foundation of character, of being a real American hero, is in the little things that you put into your "utility belt"—the tools that boys back then would have called grit, gumption, or pluck—moral fiber as a verb, if you will, or what we often here in public schools these days called the "Six Pillars of Character"—trustworthiness, respect, responsibility, fairness, caring and citizenship, as well as the kind of peculiar drive and energy that marks the best of the American spirit—think Marvel Comics' Tony Stark (Ironman) and you won't be far off the mark.

Like all master storytellers, Alger's stories begin with character, the conflicts always serving to advance a character's growth. While it may seem tame against the outrageousness of novels like Suzanne Collins' The Hunger Games, it wins out over such bleak end-of-the-world scenarios in the warmth and rightness of its moral compass, which always points to True North. This is because everything in the Alger universe is founded on the traditional morality that C. S. Lewis and others have called "the Tao," a value system that everyone, everywhere in the history of the world seems to know about, although many don't practice it.

You can see this traditional morality at work all through Andy's adventures. Think back to the beginning of the story, where Andy is already on his way to a life of middle-class success, unlike Mark the Match-Boy, Ragged Dick the bootblack and other early Alger heroes. When Andy receives news that his father is in grave financial difficulty because of an act of trust and may now lose the family farm, he returns home, two weeks' shy of graduation, giving up all thought of completing his education and attending Dartmouth College in the fall.

Yet rather than let this situation be his undoing, Andy reveals his "pluck" in his intuition that this isn't the end of the story and that great things may yet come out of this seeming tragedy. There is a fascinating and mysterious quality in Andy's "wait-and-see" attitude, reminiscent of the old Eastern Taoist story "May Be":

An old farmer had worked his crops for many years. One day his horse ran away. Upon hearing the news, his neighbors came to visit. "Such bad luck," they said sympathetically.

"May be," the farmer replied.

185

The next morning the horse returned, bringing with it three other wild horses. "How wonderful," the neighbors exclaimed.

"May be," replied the old man.

The following day, his son tried to ride one of the untamed horses, was thrown, and broke his leg. The neighbors again came to offer their sympathy on his misfortune.

"May be," answered the farmer.

The day after, military officials came to the village to draft young men into the army. Seeing that the son's leg was broken, they passed him by. The neighbors congratulated the farmer on how well things had turned out.

"May be," said the farmer.

Our Western Christian tradition likewise can speak to this deep insight, as seen in Julian of Norwich's famous words that "It behoved that there should be sin, yet all shall be well, and all shall be well, and all manner of things shall be well." At each stage of Andy's journey—from his dealings with Conrad at the boat race through to his final triumph over Squire Carter—Alger keeps us on the edge of our seat, almost but not quite astonished at Andy's persevering "wait and see" attitude.

The "payoff," for both Andy and the reader, isn't about "rags-to-riches," as people so often stereotype Alger. The author is very explicit about this: "'Business is business!'" [said Squire Carter.] These words are used as an excuse for a great many mean acts" (ch. 37). Virtue always trumps money in Alger's world. It's not the gold standard but the standard of the Golden Rule that flies on the ramparts for Alger's heroes. Nowhere is this more apparent than when Andy is able to help the poor Mrs. Carter and her family:

Andy felt a warm glow in his heart at the thought of the happiness he had been instrumental in bringing to the poor family. He had learned the great lesson that some never learn -- that there is nothing so satisfactory as helping others. We should have a much better world if that was generally understood (ch. 36).

The temptation here, especially in our own day, is to think of Alger as a mere moralist. Perhaps we have allowed ourselves to become so immersed in a culture of irony—of undercutting all genuine beliefs and emotions—that we've forgotten some of the most important things.

I would argue that Alger's novels, like faith, are meant to be "caught," not "taught." At the outset of Ch. 1, we are told that Andy "was an excellent Latin and Greek scholar," and one of the classics he undoubtedly would have translated was Horace's Ars Poetica or "The Art of Poetry." In that essay, which has influenced countless generations, Horace writes, "He has gained every vote who has mingled profit with pleasure by delighting the reader at once and instructing him."

Ours is an age that has largely lost sight of this crucial understanding of the function of art. For Horace, "profit" (by which he meant moral instruction) and "pleasure" (by which he meant happiness) always go together, like two sides of a coin. This is why Alger's books were sought out with such enthusiasm by the boys of his own day and why they still have something incredible to say to us today. "Rags-to-riches" is about spiritual riches more than material ones, both then and now.

Mark Irwin received his Ph.D. in literature and religion at the University of Virginia and has spent his time since teaching the love of great books to inner-city sixth-, seventh- and eighth-graders.

THE LIFE AND THEMES OF
HORATIO ALGER, JR.

By Stefan Kanfer

The Merriam-Webster Dictionary devotes one sentence to him: "Of, relating to, or resembling the fiction of Horatio Alger in which success is achieved through self-reliance and hard work."

True as far as it goes, but that sentence reveals nothing about the man or his accomplishment. Then again, other contemporary reference books are just as terse. Not one acknowledges that Alger in his day (circa 1880-1920) was a publishing phenomenon. During those decades, when a sale of 10,000 volumes was deemed a triumph, readers bought more than 200 million copies of Alger's works, placing him in a league with J.K. Rowling and Stephen King.

Alas, today most of his novels—and there are more than 100—are out of print. But not for long. Thanks to the resuscitation efforts of Sumner Books, a division of Creators Syndicate, Alger's best literary productions are being furnished with fresh covers, new fonts and energetic promotion.

Seldom has there been a more relevant illustration of the maxim that what goes around comes around. At the turn of the 19th century, Alger was the standard-bearer of a phenomenally successful experiment in social reform and personal improvement. That movement inspired disadvantaged kids to move on up, leading juvenile delinquents into productive, significant lives. Men as different as Groucho Marx and Ernest Hemingway were fans.

"Horatio Alger's books conveyed a powerful message to me," wrote Marx, "and to many of my young friends as well—that if you worked hard at your trade, the big chance would eventually come. As a child I didn't regard it as a myth, and as an old man I think of it as the story of my life."

Hemingway's sister Marcelline recalled that during their childhood, "There was one summer when Ernest couldn't get enough of Horatio Alger." Not that Alger's boys' books influenced Papa's prose style. But there must have been something in the writer's stress on grit and self-reliance that affected young Ernest, as it did so many of his contemporaries.

By the end of the Roaring Twenties, though, Horatio Alger had become as passé as the Ford Model T. During the Depression he fared no better; Nathaniel West's satirical 1934 novel, A Cool Million, sent Alger's plots in reverse, as the naïve protagonist loses limb after limb seeking success among rapacious capitalists. Decades later, the film adaptation of Hunter Thompson's 1971 novel, Fear and Loathing in Las Vegas, presented the antihero as "Horatio Alger gone mad on drugs in Las Vegas."

What lay behind Alger's ability to enchant so many Americans—and to enrage so many others? The author's story furnishes a trove of clues:

The sickly child of a Unitarian minister in Marlborough, Massachusetts, Horatio, born in 1832, was always the smallest in his class and far from an academic star. Still, his report cards were good enough for admission to Harvard. There his academic prowess was in inverse proportion to his size (5 feet 2 inches). He won prizes, published verse and fiction in undergraduate magazines, and labeled the entire four years a period of "unmixed happiness."

Decades would pass before he found such contentment again. Upon graduation, Horatio attempted to make his way as a writer. After five unsuccessful years, he returned to Harvard, this time to study at the Divinity School. In 1860 the Reverend Horatio Alger was named minister of the First Parish Unitarian Church of Brewster on Cape Cod. Salary: $800 per year. To supplement his meager income, he turned once again to writing. This time, his stories were well-received, and he allowed himself to dream of a dual career of preacher and writer. That's when catastrophe struck.

It was of his own making, if one historian is to be believed. According to this claim, a 13-year-old told his parents that the new parson had made advances to him. An investigation began. Another lad made a similar complaint. Faced with charges of behaving inappropriately, the accused was allowed to resign—with the proviso that he leave town at once.

Sometime later, Horatio wrote a poem about one Friar Anselmo, who had committed an unspecified crime. Melancholy and remorseful, he comes across a wounded traveler and gives him aid. Whereupon an angel materializes and offers salvation:

Thy guilty stains shall be washed white again
By noble service done thy fellow man.

The fugitive repaired to New York City in the spring of 1866, resolved to live out the Christian ideal, expiating his sin by saving others. The Manhattan he entered was the epicenter of the Gilded Age, a magnet for millions of ambitious climbers, drawn by the post-Civil War boom. Out of sight of the glittering prosperity, the mansions and carriages, however, was another New York, a squalid night town that travelers compared to Calcutta, India.

In The Good Old Days, They Were Terrible, historian Otto Bettmann reports that there was scarcely a slum that pedestrians could negotiate "without climbing over a heap of trash or, in rain, wading through a bed of slime." Many streets were so dangerous that policemen hesitated to walk them alone. A Gramercy Park resident noted in his diary, "Most of my friends are investing in revolvers and carry them about at night"—and the Park was one of the city's better neighborhoods.

The New York City street urchin entered the national consciousness in those years. More than 60,000 neglected or abandoned kids ran unsupervised in the street, partly because of the fallout from the tidal waves of immigration from Europe and partly because of families broken by the Civil War.

What was to be done about these juveniles likely to die on the streets or to end up behind bars? The Reverend Charles Loring Brace founded the Children's Aid Society, designed to take homeless or abused kids away from their corrosive environments. At the same time, John Hughes, New York's first Roman Catholic archbishop, set up parochial schools and a residential institution called the Catholic Protectory, which brought up abandoned or orphaned children to be useful members of society.

Horatio Alger joined these efforts at reclamation. He, too, asked himself what could be done about homeless children. Seeking answers, he wandered through the city's worst neighborhoods. He interviewed "street arabs" who spoke of broken homes, violent confrontations with parents, doomed futures. He observed how their cocky attitudes masked a profound despair. He advised them to get real jobs instead of hanging about, squandering whatever came their way from shining shoes or picking pockets. A handful nodded in agreement, expressing the desire to change their lives; most were content to take life as they found it.

Why, he pondered, did individuals subjected to the same conditions turn out so differently? One boy might become a thief, a sociopath, even a killer. His neighbor, perhaps his brother, might aim to be an upright citizen. What was the difference between them?

What saved certain boys, he came to believe, was a quality that gave them the strength to resist sloth and temptation. In a word, character. But was this inborn? In that case determinism won the day, and change was out of the question. Or, given the right opportunity and attitude, could a dispossessed youth win his share of the American dream? The latter, Alger believed—but only if the boy stopped regarding himself as a victim.

As Alger meditated upon the worst crime of the slums—the stealing of childhood from children—an idea came to him. He would be Brother Anselmo redivivus. He had sinned against youths; now he would rescue them—and in the process save himself. As the novelist put it, by depicting the situation of city waifs, he would "excite a deeper and more widespread sympathy in the public mind, as well as exert a salutary influence upon the class of whom he is writing, by setting before them inspiring examples of what energy, ambition, and an honest purpose may achieve."

Ragged Dick became the template of the fiction to follow. Subtitled Street Life in New York with the Boot Blacks, it charted the rise of a 14-year-old boy from poverty to prosperity. Dick Hunter is an adolescent with all odds against him. He has no family, he smokes, drinks alcohol when he can afford it—not very often on the small change he gets from shining gentlemen's shoes—and sleeps on gratings in the winter.

Yet something separates him from his fellow waifs. He refuses to pick pockets like the others, won't mock his elders, and yearns to "grow up 'spectable.'" His bearing and his innate decency attract the attention of upright New Yorkers. One introduces him to his church; another presents Dick with a few dollars.

The earnest youth resolves to become literate to save his money and live a clean life. One day on a walk near South Ferry he sees a toddler fall in the water. Without hesitation, Dick jumps in and saves the drowning child. In gratitude, the father, an affluent businessman, offers the rescuer a job in his office. Gainfully employed, the onetime vagabond Dick Hunter becomes Richard Hunter Esq., and shuts the door forever on the "old vagabond life which he hoped never to resume."

Naïve? Simplistic? To the jaded, the cynical and the ignorant, yes. But not to thousands of children trapped in the real world of poverty and early death. They got the message of Ragged Dick and demanded more Horatio Alger novels with more moral lessons for them to absorb. Those books changed—and in many cases saved—lives a century before Dr. Martin Luther King Jr. stated his belief that what mattered was not the color of one's skin but the content of one's character.

Today, if you listen closely you can hear, amid the jeers, the escalating sound of the last laugh. In 1947, the Horatio Alger Association was founded. It attracts more prominent men and women now than it did then. The group is dedicated to recognizing American leaders who rose, like Alger's young heroes, from humble origins "through honesty, hard work, self-reliance and perseverance." With grants to U.S. high-school students who have "faced and overcome great obstacles in their young lives," the association encourages them to emulate such enterprising and disparate members as Oprah Winfrey and Ray Kroc, Tom Brokaw and Maya Angelou, Stan Musial and Colin Powell.

They can all testify to the truths that lie between the covers of this volume. Turn the first few pages, and you'll understand why so many followed Horatio Alger's breathless, cliff-hanging chapters leading the way from skid row to success. And why so many more are about to read that map in a world where everything has changed—except the basic truths of life.

Stefan Kanfer is an award-winning writer for City Journal and the author of numerous best-selling books.

ABOUT HORATIO ALGER, JR.

Horatio Alger was born in 1832 in Chelsea, Massachusetts. He spent his early years in the small town and under the guidance of the church and his father, the town pastor, before the family moved just west of Boston to the town of Marlborough. As a shy young boy, Alger poured himself into books and soon became a distinguished student. He studied at Harvard and Harvard Divinity School before becoming a minister. He practiced ministry for a few years near Boston and on Cape Cod, but he was distracted by his true passion: writing. He loved to write, and by 1865 Alger had written a handful of stories, including Frank's Campaign and Paul Prescott's Charge. The latter was the first in a series of stories that would eventually lead to his great success. In 1866, Alger moved to New York to write poetry, newspaper stories and magazine articles. However, he was shocked to find so many homeless and forgotten children among the streets, an unfortunate consequence of the Civil War. He made it his duty to aid the condition of these lost children, both through his stories and by his continuous acts of benevolence.

Horatio Alger became a household name shortly after the Civil War when he began publishing stories in the form of serializations. These serializations were featured in magazines such as Student and Schoolmate and were later compiled as books. Alger's books became enormously popular, especially among teenage boys across the country, and they soon reached millions and millions of readers. Alger continued to produce several stories a year, and, in later years, wrote novels in and of themselves instead of novels from magazine serials.

The years immediately following the Civil War were the same years when the United States emerged as one nation on the road to becoming a worldwide empire. The years between 1865 and 1900 were the years of the empire builders, with the rags-to-riches stories of John D. Rockefeller, Andrew Carnegie, Cornelius Vanderbilt and Thomas Edison. They were the years that laid the foundation for Henry Ford and other business titans and for the spectacular growth of the American economy throughout the 20th century and through today. During these years, Alger published well over 100 stories, poems and novels that spoke to the timeless themes and successes of this era.

The theme of Alger's books is consistent: If you work hard, go the extra mile, are faithful and honest, show kindness and generosity, and maintain a cheerful, positive and optimistic attitude, you will succeed in creating financial security and happiness. On the other hand, if you lie, cheat, steal, are lazy or envious, and try to take advantage of other people, you will be doomed to failure and misery. Despite his background as a preacher, Alger does not make these points in a self-righteous or pontificating way. What he does instead -- just like the parables that Jesus told -- is to create stories that illustrate the virtues that lead to success. And the stories that Alger creates are no ordinary stories. Each one is filled with lively plots and twists and turns, ones that are always unexpected and keep the reader wanting to know what's going to happen next.

As Alger grew older, he continuously strived to write the Great American Novel, little realizing that the rags-to-riches stories he created were more influential than any other novelists'. He travelled out west in early 1877 searching for new material and returned near the end of the year, producing similar stories with a new western backdrop. By 1897, Alger was suffering from asthma, bronchitis and slight short-term memory loss. He moved in with his sister in South Natick, Massachusetts where he spent the last two years of his life.

Most people have never heard of Horatio Alger while some are vaguely familiar with the term "rags-to-riches." In the Alger family, it was the norm to burn correspondence and manuscripts, and this, coupled with Alger's shyness, has greatly kept him from history's limelight. Though too often forgotten today, Alger's works and the themes within them still affect the American psyche. Many assert that there is a lagging spirit in present American culture, that these inspiring stories are irrelevant. Young people are bombarded with external stimuli that make it difficult for them to get to know themselves. Wide-eyed innocence and childlike enthusiasm, once revered as admirable qualities, are sources of mockery and disdain, which makes cynicism and pessimism inevitable. Video games, television shows, movies and music are all aimed at titillating and at seeing who can be the most gritty, violent or shocking. More than a few commentators have used the word "degrading" to describe the assault that children encounter today.

This is unfortunate. Young people need heroes and role models today just as much as they did in the 1870s and '80s, when Alger was creating them at a feverish pace from his New York City apartment, writing as many as four books at a time. Publisher A.K. Loring asserted that Alger's books "captured the spirits of reborn America" for "above all you can hear the cry of triumph of the oppressed over the oppressor ... What Alger has done is to portray the soul – the ambitious soul – of the country." Years later, biographer Edwin P. Hoyt concludes that Alger is "a writer whose influence on the American scene has been so profound that it is hard to measure." Indeed, Alger's works made an overwhelming impression on American culture and society that are still alive with us today. It is for this reason that these classics must be brought to a new generation of readers.

OUR COMMITMENT TO
HORATIO ALGER

By Rick Newcombe

Sumner Books is totally committed to reviving interest in Horatio Alger, one of the best-selling authors of all time yet someone who has been all but forgotten today. I'd like to tell you how this project came about.

Probably the best starting point is to tell you a little about myself. I grew up in suburban Chicago, and my parents were religious and fundamentally optimistic in their outlook on life. They encouraged all eight of their children to be positive in our thinking and hope and pray for the best in all situations. In my adolescence, I discovered many of the self-help authors from the 20th century, including Dale Carnegie, Napoleon Hill and Norman Vincent Peale. I remember reading a small magazine in the 1970s, when I was in my 20s, called Success Unlimited and being inspired each month to work hard and stay positive. The publisher of this magazine was W. Clement Stone, who started his career selling insurance policies door to door and who went on to build Combined Insurance, which became part of Aon, one of the largest insurance companies in the world.

By the time Mr. Stone died in 2002, he was a very successful businessman, an extremely generous philanthropist and totally committed to spreading the gospel of positive thinking. I remember reading one of his books, The Success System That Never Fails, which was both an autobiography and a blueprint for achieving success. Stone told the story of spending a summer on a farm in Michigan when he was 12, getting fresh air, helping on the farm and enjoying picnics, carnivals and camping out.

W. Clement Stone

"But I'll never forget the first day I went upstairs to the attic," he wrote, "for there I met Horatio Alger. At least 50 of his books, dusty and weather-worn, were piled in the corner. I took one down to the hammock in the front yard and started to read."

Stone said he was so enthralled he couldn't stop. "I read through all of them that summer," he wrote.

He said the principle in each book was that "the hero became a success because he was a man of character -- the villain a failure because he deceived and embezzled. How many Alger books were sold? No one knows. Estimates range from 100 million to 300 million. We do know that his books inspired thousands of American boys from poor families to strive to do the right thing because it was right and to acquire wealth."

That was the first time I had heard of Horatio Alger, but it never occurred to me to try to find his books. Over the years, I founded Creators Syndicate, which became one of the most successful newspaper syndication companies in the world. I attribute much of our success to our positive thinking and upbeat attitude. We became a multimillion-dollar international corporation by syndicating a wide variety of journalists, celebrities and award-winning cartoonists.

As we were expanding into new businesses, e-books and audiobooks were a natural starting point because we work with so many talented writers and artists. But we also wanted to try new things. With that in mind, I remembered Mr. Stone's enthusiastic recommendation of Horatio Alger's books, and I decided to read some. Many were available as e-books, and I thoroughly enjoyed them.

I had a good feeling whenever I was transported back to New York City as it was in 1870, when trains were called "cars" and there were no automobiles. There was a constant risk of crossing the streets without streetlights or walk signs. A number of years later, the Brooklyn Dodgers, now the Los Angeles Dodgers, got their name from the treacherous dodging of horses, wagons and streetcars that was required to cross the street in the city. In those days, plumbing with hot and cold running water was not taken for granted, much less radios, televisions, computers or smartphones. Are you kidding? A smartphone in the 1860s? There wasn't even a telephone.

But what great stories Alger wrote -- one after another. I couldn't get enough of them! And it was impossible not to feel grateful for all the modern conveniences of the 21st century when immersing myself in the world of America as it was in the 1860s and '70s.

As I read book after book, I felt like a teenager all over again, excited about the future and the promise of a brighter tomorrow. It was then that I decided to go full bore into spreading the word of Horatio Alger.

One of the problems with the e-books was the lack of organization; another was the maddening number of typos, over and over and over, or the lack of illustrations or the lack of a table of contents. In fact, what was intended to be a good deed to spread Mr. Alger's message really turned out to be something of a disservice.

So I made it my mission to have professional editors edit the texts so there were no typographical or spelling errors. We found appropriate illustrations. We included detailed tables of contents for each book, and we decided to publish them in groups, when appropriate, which has never been done before. We are including commentaries and teachers guides with each e-book.

We also decided to make audiobooks of as many of these "Stories of Success" as possible. We hired a terrific actor, Ben Gillman, and his initial experience shows you how far we have to go to spread the word. Ben went to the Hollywood public library to find some Horatio Alger books, but there was none. "You'd have to go to the downtown public library, in the historical section, to find those," the librarian told him.

Remember, this is one of the best-selling American authors of all time, yet it is as if he never existed.

Part of the problem is that some of the caricatures of Horatio Alger over the years have been absolutely brutal. Even to this day, the Encyclopedia Britannica, from which we expect objective reporting, calls Alger's dialogue and plots "outrageously bad." Come again? The encyclopedia is supposed to provide broad knowledge on specific subjects, not offer the biased literary criticism of a handful of editors. Talk about being unfair -- and just plain wrong!

How do you answer a cheap shot like that? Really, it is nothing more than an incredibly snooty opinion; in fact, it is an "outrageously bad" opinion. Remember, the Horatio Alger books were intended to be not great literature but rather inspirational stories to motivate young boys to achieve a better life. If the dialogue and plots were not lively and believable, the books would not have sold in the millions. The fact that Horatio Alger helped form the American character shows that an incredible number of boys ate up his books as thrilling and believable.

The brilliant writer Stefan Kanfer wrote an extensive review of Horatio Alger's works in 2000 for City Journal magazine, a publication of the prestigious Manhattan Institute. He started off believing the critics, but when he actually read some of Horatio Alger's books, he drew a totally different conclusion. "I began reading the novels aloud to my children," he wrote. "We found them well-plotted, entertaining, and instructive, not at all the righteous antiquities that I had been led to believe. Almost every chapter ends with a cliff-hanger, and all of us could hardly wait for the next night to find out what happened. The conclusions never failed to produce an emotional satisfaction and a feeling that what the author was selling -- independence, forbearance, square dealing -- was well worth buying."

We can only speculate about why the critics have been so harsh on Horatio Alger, but no doubt some it stems from their being turned off by precisely the character traits that Mr. Kanfer identifies. Like it or not, there is a mindset that scoffs at individual achievement through hard work, a positive attitude and generosity -- living every day with an "attitude of gratitude," which is the essence of Horatio Alger's message.

W. Clement Stone was routinely mocked for starting the day by saying, "I feel healthy! I feel happy! I feel terrific!" He encouraged his employees to do the same. In fact, he encouraged everyone to demonstrate outward enthusiasm and PMA, which stood for a positive mental attitude. His critics thought he was ridiculous, but Mr. Stone got the last laugh, living to age 100, which he had set as his goal, and accumulating hundreds of millions of dollars.

Roswell Crawford is an important character in Ragged Dick and Fame and Fortune because he oozes the world-owes-me-a-living attitude that is so common today. "Roswell was troubled with a large share of pride," Alger writes, "though it might have troubled himself to explain what he had to be proud of."

Roswell never understands the importance of integrity and its relationship to earning one's living. In fact, he once says that he would be happy to be paid $10 a week for nothing. "Well, if I get it, I don't care if I don't earn it," he says. In fact, Roswell is ashamed to be seen in the streets carrying a large bundle as part of a delivery for his job. Before being fired, his boss tells him, "You appear to think yourself of too great consequence to discharge properly the duties of your position."

Contrast that with Richard Hunter's attitude toward his entry-level job when he first starts working at the firm. "I'm ready to do anything that is required of me. I want to make myself useful," he says.

I have the impression that was the same attitude that Horatio Alger had as he approached his goal of becoming a successful writer who could change the world -- or at least the world of the thousands of homeless street urchins in the big city. It is difficult to imagine how bad their plight was. For instance, in 1874, which was seven years after Ragged Dick was first published, there was a little girl named Mary Ellen Wilson, who was beaten unmercifully by her stepmother. She was sent out into the streets ill-clothed in winter. There were other abuses, and they were horrible.

So a social worker named Etta Angel Wheeler wanted to intervene, to help get the child out of that environment. But there were no laws to protect children in such situations. Etta was desperate -- and clever. She enlisted the help of the American Society for the Prevention of Cruelty to Animals because animals were protected by law. Her attorneys argued that Mary Ellen, "as a member of the animal kingdom, deserved the same protection as abused animals." This led to new legislation and various child protective services.

Horatio Alger was at the forefront of this movement. He wanted to help the poor kids in the inner city, and he wound up not only helping them but inspiring millions of other young readers across the country. Many of them transformed their lives as a direct result of the inspiration of the "Stories of Success" that Horatio Alger managed to tell in one exciting setting after another.

It is not surprising that Ernest Hemingway's sister said that her brother could not get enough of Horatio Alger or that Walter Brennan, a famous actor for much of the 20th century, devoured his books. As the legendary Groucho Marx said: "Horatio Alger's books conveyed a powerful message to me and to many of my young friends -- that if you worked hard at your trade, the big chance would eventually come. As a child, I didn't regard it as a myth, and as an old man, I think of it as the story of my life."

Groucho was speaking for millions of Americans in the past and, we hope, millions more in the future.

Rick Newcombe is the founder and CEO of Creators Syndicate, Creators Publishing and Sumner Books.

PREVIEW OF ANOTHER ADVENTURE IN THE HORATIO ALGER "STORIES OF SUCCESS" SERIES

Ragged Dick

By Horatio Alger, Jr.

"Wake up there, youngster," said a rough voice.

Ragged Dick opened his eyes slowly, and stared stupidly in the face of the speaker, but did not offer to get up.

"Wake up, you young vagabond!" said the man a little impatiently;

"I suppose you'd lay there all day, if I hadn't called you."

"What time is it?" asked Dick.

"Seven o'clock."

"Seven o'clock! I oughter've been up an hour ago. I know what 'twas made me so precious sleepy. I went to the Old Bowery last night, and didn't turn in till past twelve."

"You went to the Old Bowery? Where'd you get your money?" asked the man, who was a porter in the employ of a firm doing business on Spruce Street. "Made it by shines, in course. My guardian don't allow me no money for theatres, so I have to earn it."

"Some boys get it easier than that," said the porter significantly.

"You don't catch me stealin', if that's what you mean," said Dick.

"Don't you ever steal, then?"

"No, and I wouldn't. Lots of boys does it, but I wouldn't."

"Well, I'm glad to hear you say that. I believe there's some good in you, Dick, after all."

"Oh, I'm a rough customer!" said Dick. "But I wouldn't steal. It's mean."

"I'm glad you think so, Dick," and the rough voice sounded gentler than at first. "Have you got any money to buy your breakfast?"

"No, but I'll soon get some."

While this conversation had been going on, Dick had got up. His bedchamber had been a wooden box half full of straw, on which the young boot-black had reposed his weary limbs, and slept as soundly as if it had been a bed of down. He dumped down into the straw without taking the trouble of undressing.

A bootblack working in New York City.

Getting up too was an equally short process. He jumped out of the box, shook himself, picked out one or two straws that had found their way into rents in his clothes, and, drawing a well-worn cap over his uncombed locks, he was all ready for the business of the day.

Dick's appearance as he stood beside the box was rather peculiar. His pants were torn in several places, and had apparently belonged in the first instance to a boy two sizes larger than himself. He wore a vest, all the buttons of which were gone except two, out of which peeped a shirt which looked as if it had been worn a month. To complete his costume he wore a coat too long for him, dating back, if one might judge from its general appearance, to a remote antiquity.

Washing the face and hands is usually considered proper in commencing the day, but Dick was above such refinement. He had no particular dislike to dirt, and did not think it necessary to remove several dark streaks on his face and hands. But in spite of his dirt and rags there was something about Dick that was attractive. It was easy to see that if he had been clean and well dressed he would have been decidedly good-looking. Some of his companions were sly, and their faces inspired distrust; but Dick had a frank, straight-forward manner that made him a favorite.

Dick's business hours had commenced. He had no office to open. His little blacking-box was ready for use, and he looked sharply in the faces of all who passed, addressing each with, "Shine yer boots, sir?"

"How much?" asked a gentleman on his way to his office.

"Ten cents," said Dick, dropping his box, and sinking upon his knees on the sidewalk, flourishing his brush with the air of one skilled in his profession.

"Ten cents! Isn't that a little steep?"

"Well, you know 'taint all clear profit," said Dick, who had already set to work. "There's the blacking costs something, and I have to get a new brush pretty often."

"And you have a large rent too," said the gentleman quizzically, with a glance at a large hole in Dick's coat.

"Yes, sir," said Dick, always ready to joke; "I have to pay such a big rent for my manshun up on Fifth Avenoo, that I can't afford to take less than ten cents a shine. I'll give you a bully shine, sir."

"Be quick about it, for I am in a hurry. So your house is on Fifth Avenue, is it?"

It isn't anywhere else," said Dick, and Dick spoke the truth there.

"What tailor do you patronize?" asked the gentleman, surveying Dick's attire.

"Would you like to go to the same one?" asked Dick, shrewdly.

"Well, no; it strikes me that he didn't give you a very good fit."

"This coat once belonged to General Washington," said Dick, comically. "He wore it all through the Revolution, and it got torn some, 'cause he fit so hard. When he died he told his widder to give it to some smart young feller that hadn't got none of his own; so she gave it to me. But if you'd like it, sir, to remember General Washington by, I'll let you have it reasonable."

"Thank you, but I wouldn't want to deprive you of it. And did your pants come from General Washington too?"

"No, they was a gift from Lewis Napoleon. Lewis had outgrown 'em and sent 'em to me—he's bigger than me, and that's why they don't fit."

"It seems you have distinguished friends. Now, my lad, I suppose you would like your money."

"I shouldn't have any objection," said Dick.

"I believe," said the gentleman, examining his wallet, "I haven't got anything short of twenty-five cents. Have you got any change?"

"Not a cent," said Dick. "All my money's invested in the Erie Railroad."

"That's unfortunate."

"Shall I get the money changed, sir?"

"I can't wait; I've got to meet an appointment immediately. I'll hand you twenty-five cents, and you can leave the change at my office any time during the day."

"All right, sir. Where is it?"

"No. 125 Fulton Street. Shall you remember?"

"Yes, sir. What name?"

"Greyson—office on second floor."

"All right, sir; I'll bring it."

"I wonder whether the little scamp will prove honest," said Mr. Greyson to himself, as he walked away. "If he does, I'll give him my custom regularly. If he don't as is most likely, I shan't mind the loss of fifteen cents."

Dick always jokes about having Erie Railroad shares, but doesn't actually have them. This is what they would look like if he did have them.

Mr. Greyson didn't understand Dick. Our ragged hero wasn't a model boy in all respects. I am afraid he swore sometimes, and now and then he played tricks upon unsophisticated boys from the country, or gave a wrong direction to honest old gentlemen unused to the city. A clergyman in search of the Cooper Institute he once directed to the Tombs Prison, and, following him unobserved, was highly delighted when the unsuspicious stranger walked up the front steps of the great stone building on Centre Street, and tried to obtain admission.

"I guess he wouldn't want to stay long if he did get in," thought Ragged Dick, hitching up his pants. "Leastways I shouldn't. They're so precious glad to see you that they won't let you go, but board you gratooitous, and never send in no bills."

Another of Dick's faults was his extravagance. Being always wide-awake and ready for business, he earned enough to have supported him comfortably and respectably. There were not a few young clerks who employed Dick from time to time in his professional capacity, who scarcely earned as much as he, greatly as their style and dress exceeded his. But Dick was careless of his earnings. Where they went he could hardly have told himself. However much he managed to earn during the day, all was generally spent before morning. He was fond of going to the Old Bowery Theatre, and to Tony Pastor's, and if he had any money left afterwards, he would invite some of his friends in somewhere to have an oyster-stew; so it seldom happened that he commenced the day with a penny.

The Bowery Theater, which is one of the places where Dick would spend his money.

Then I am sorry to add that Dick had formed the habit of smoking. This cost him considerable, for Dick was rather fastidious about his cigars, and wouldn't smoke the cheapest. Besides, having a liberal nature, he was generally ready to treat his companions. But of course the expense was the smallest objection. No boy of fourteen can smoke without being affected injuriously. Men are frequently injured by smoking, and boys always. But large numbers of the newsboys and boot-blacks form the habit. Exposed to the cold and wet they find that it warms them up, and the self-indulgence grows upon them. It is not uncommon to see a little boy, too young to be out of his mother's sight, smoking with all the apparent satisfaction of a veteran smoker.

There was another way in which Dick sometimes lost money. There was a noted gambling-house on Baxter Street, which in the evening was sometimes crowded with these juvenile gamesters, who staked their hard earnings, generally losing of course, and refreshing themselves from time to time with a vile mixture of liquor at two cents a glass. Sometimes Dick strayed in here, and played with the rest.

I have mentioned Dick's faults and defects, because I want it understood, to begin with, that I don't consider him a model boy. But there were some good points about him nevertheless. He was above doing anything mean or dishonorable. He would not steal, or cheat, or impose upon younger boys, but was frank and straight-forward, manly and self-reliant. His nature was a noble one, and had saved him from all mean faults. I hope my young readers will like him as I do, without being blind to his faults. Perhaps, although he was only a boot-black, they may find something in him to imitate.

And now, having fairly introduced Ragged Dick to my young readers,

I must refer them to the next chapter for his further adventures.

BE SURE TO LISTEN TO THE
AUDIOBOOK "STORIES OF SUCCESS"
SERIES BY HORATIO ALGER,
AVAILABLE ON AUDIBLE.COM AND
ITUNES. GO TO
WWW.SUMNERBOOKS.COM.

www.ingramcontent.com/pod-product-compliance
Lightning Source LLC
Chambersburg PA
CBHW070829120626
46556CB00002B/690

* 9 7 8 1 9 3 9 1 0 4 1 7 5 *